The Only
Study
Guide
You'll Ever
Need

The Only
Study
Guide
You'll Ever
Need

Jade Bowler

BLINK
bringing you closer

First published in the UK by Blink Publishing
An imprint of Bonnier Books UK
4th Floor, Victoria House, Bloomsbury Square, London, WC1B 4DA
Owned by Bonnier Books
Sveavägen 56, Stockholm, Sweden

Hardback – 978-1-78870-419-9
Ebook – 978-1-78870-420-5

A CIP catalogue of this book is available from the British Library.

Designed by IDSUK (Data Connection) Ltd
Graphs and diagrams by Envy Designs Ltd
Illustrations by Sophie McDonnell
Printed and bound by Clays Ltd, Elcograf S.p.A

3 5 7 9 10 8 6 4 2

Every reasonable effort has been made to trace copyright holders of material
reproduced in this book, but if any have been inadvertently overlooked the
publishers would be glad to hear from them.

Blink Publishing is an imprint of Bonnier Books UK
www.bonnierbooks.co.uk

For my YouTube audience,
who somehow managed to make a very ordinary
girl feel extraordinary.
You are always my casual magic.

CONTENTS

INTRODUCTION

Welcome. I have a secret: I know something about you.

I don't know your name. I don't know your life story. But what do I know? I know you care.

Whether you believe it or not, you care about your education, your future and your learning. You see, whether it was shoved in your hands by an eager parent or ordered online in a time of crisis, you picked up this book and made it to this first page and that means you want to take charge of your education. You decided to invest your free time in reflecting on how you study, which is so bloody cool!

Being a teen is hard. Genuinely, I salute you. The education system seems to forget that there are hundred other things going on in our lives besides just school. You might be working a job to support your family. You might be juggling friendship drama. You might be figuring out your identity (which is a full-time job in itself!). Mental health is just overlooked when it comes to productivity. If you're battling dark clouds in your brain, how could school ever be the number one priority? Which is why this book is not a one-size-fits-all approach. This book welcomes the multi faceted you and is an invitation to motivate yourself to achieve whatever academic goals you want to have, whether that's turning your predicted As into A*s, or finding a reason to smash a pass in that subject you hate. I've done my best to make this book fun, accessible and actually helpful. I've drawn on examples in my life that helped me slay the exam system and explained techniques that I *wish* someone had taught me. You don't have to dig into the primary literature of the neuroscience of learning – I've done the basics for you.

My name is Jade and I'm a 20-year-old British university student. I achieved all A*s (8s and 9s) in my GCSEs and all A*s in my A levels. However, that doesn't make me an expert. I do not have a PhD in study methods or any other official credentials. In fact, neither of my parents went to university and as I'm the oldest child, I was the guinea pig – I didn't have older siblings who could share their wisdom with me. That's sort of what I hope I can be for you. So this is a guide for students written not by a teacher, a professor or an academic – instead by someone who has been through the process recently and who loves learning. It includes all the realistic tips and tricks I wish I'd known a few years ago. If I can make it through the system and not only survive, but learn to thrive, you can too.

I went to a state school just outside London where I felt very uncool for liking learning. I watched many of my peers give up before they even started and saw teachers come and go, sometimes leaving mid-way through the exam year. In other words, my school was hardly the peak of academia.

But I've always cared a lot about learning and I decided early on that I was really going to try. For, as many flaws as the UK education system has, I'm so grateful that we have the chance to learn. I knew I had a choice: to coast along and be done with it or to tighten my laces, shove my curls behind my ears and work out how to be more efficient. I chose the latter.

I was an extremely stressed GCSE student. For those years, I lived in a bubble of pressure from teachers, parents and peers. It was only after I finished my exams that I realised I had been worried for nothing. There were so many things I wish I'd learned earlier – everything from achieving the right mindset to how to tackle all the content. I began to mentor younger students and it was fulfilling to share my knowledge and help others.

When I was doing my GCSEs, I'd headed to YouTube looking for just that sort of helping hand. All I wanted was advice from older students who had gone through it already to put me at ease. There was nothing. As someone who wasn't into traditional YouTube culture, I was the last person my friends expected to start a channel and yet there I was, suddenly convinced that I had something the internet needed to hear.

I saved up for a camera for a year, split half the cost with my parents as a Christmas present and felt like I'd found the missing piece to something bigger. Alongside studying for my A levels, I spent two months teaching myself how to edit. In February 2017, I started my YouTube channel 'UnJaded Jade', driven by the need to share my experiences and create an online space for students to relate to others.

My videos follow my academic journey, share honest tips and advice for navigating our school system and, ultimately, try to inspire a positive mindset where anyone can achieve anything they want. The response I have received over the years has been overwhelming. I get hundreds of messages every day from students who feel more in control of their education.

YouTube utterly changed my life, when all I wanted was for it to change those of others.

I've always dreamed of compiling my advice into one guide. One that encompasses not only effective revision techniques but the nuances of being a successful, genuinely happy student in whatever academic system you're in.

This is a story of productivity and motivation. I made lots of mistakes when I was studying and I have explained them here so you don't have to make them. This is what school never teaches you: how to revise *properly* and how to not burn out.

As I say, I really am no expert. But I do know what worked for me. Maybe it'll work for you too.

How to Use

The beauty of this book is that it is not mine, it is yours, and you can use it however you want. If you have a bit of time, I recommend reading it from start to finish because the chapters build on one another. But if you're crunched for time, or desperate to work out how timetables work, skip through the pages to your heart's content; I won't judge. Daringly turn to that chapter you need and inhale it until you can breathe new life into how you study.

What I do ask is this: Come into each chapter not as a passive museum-goer at an art exhibition. Don't admire the words and smile at the techniques and agree that it sounds good.

Be the artist. Use the chapters as inspiration to prod your own life, to redraw your systems and to create new ways of doing things. Stop after each chapter and answer the 'Put it in Practice' questions. Go back and reread chapters once you've tried applying them. Reflect on how you view your place in the academic system and the level of pressure you put on yourself. Enter this book and be active, because that is how you will grow. This book is what you make of it.

I'm honoured you're here.

CHAPTER 1

MOTIVATION

When I got a D in my first A level chemistry test, I convinced myself that it was bad luck. Even when I spent all night on a simple homework task, I told myself that it would get better. It was only when I got a U in my next test that I almost dropped chemistry on the spot. It was one month into Year 12 and the rose-tinted glasses of a student back from the summer holidays had faded with the snap of every sheet of paper I added to my ring-binder folder.

I was taking A level chemistry, biology, maths and English literature. Chemistry became the bane of my life. Not only is the subject extremely difficult but we were given a brand new teacher. Despite her efforts, I learned nothing. Her explanations tangled the textbook in my mind like a maze and sometimes she wouldn't show up to lessons. It was a mess.

I can remember coming home one day, getting out my home-work and feeling sick to my stomach that I understood nothing. I was spending triple the time on chemistry than I was on any other subject.

I received my first chemistry test back. I could see the red marks on the paper before it got to me. Right there, in a bold scribble: D. This is not an awful grade in itself but I was gutted. After scoring highly in chemistry GCSE and spending hours revising only to get most questions wrong, it was a demoralising start to A levels.

When I got home, the last thing I wanted to do was look at my test paper. I still didn't understand the content. My teacher couldn't explain it in a way that made sense to me and seeing that D grade bordering on a U was enough to convince me I should reconsider taking chemistry after all.

After two months of failing to understand anything, I over-thought myself into a place of extreme unmotivation because it felt like an invisible contract had been broken. We place so much faith in our teachers to know what they're doing in order to make us feel like we have a chance. A good teacher is like a row of lights illuminating a dark pathway. Teachers don't walk the road for you, but rather point you through the twists and turns in a way that makes you feel like the destination is in reach. Without them, the path is dark. It's easy to stop walking. The next few weeks, I didn't use my free periods to study. I hung out with friends and I didn't keep my revision resources up to date. It didn't shock me when I continued to understand nothing in chemistry. My teacher would ask the class questions and receive blank stares. We complained to the science department but my school didn't have the resources to change teachers or support us further.

I got my second chemistry test back. This time, it was even worse: I had achieved a U. By this point, I could feel my class losing all hope in this subject. Dismissals of, 'This is gibberish', 'If Miss can't understand it, how am I meant to?' and 'These questions are just unfair' filled the room.

By the time my third chemistry test rolled around, I needed a turning point. I was at home, revisiting my flashcards, when it hit me for the first time that I couldn't keep blaming my teacher. In the grand scheme of my life, when anyone asked for my chemistry A level grade they wouldn't care who taught me or how 'unfair' the questions were. They'd just see my grade. So if a good teacher is the light on a dark path, I needed to create my own torch. I emailed the head of chemistry that day.

I requested a weekly meeting to go over anything I hadn't understood. I would stay behind after school if the head of chemistry would too and go over every test question I got wrong until it clicked. She didn't reply to my email, so I went to see her in the staff room as a last chance glimpse of hope. She had to agree.

Starting that Tuesday, I visited her after school. The difference this made was huge. In being proactive, I was essentially telling myself, week in, week out, that I would make this chemistry thing work. Whatever I didn't understand, I could and would understand with a bit more effort. This involved finding every online resource for A Level chemistry and inhaling it. I started reading about self-improvement and tools for sustained motivation through good habits. I researched the science of learning and radically changed my revision methods. My bedroom walls became a vision board of Post-it notes of things I committed to understand. I began to change my mindset towards mistakes because I finally realised that getting something wrong meant that I could get it right in the future.

In my next chemistry test, I got an A. I almost cried.

My chemistry class went from 21 people to just eight by Year 13. The AS exam was too hard and most of us failed, meaning over half the class had to retake the year. Let me tell you, it would have been so much easier to give up chemistry at the start of

Year 12. Would I have saved myself some tears? Yes. Would I have struggled less? Sure. But there is nothing more satisfying than finally understanding something you know is difficult. Even when you face setbacks in terms of lack of support or changes to specifications, keep struggling. The moment it all clicks is one worth fighting for.

I got an A* in A level chemistry. I am so proud of that grade.

Imagine it's results day. You're at school, surrounded by nervous peers and grinning teachers, with whom you avoid eye contact. Maybe your parents are with you. Maybe they're even more invested than you are. Pressure is in the air, the people and in that envelope. You find your name and take it.

When you hold that all-important envelope, what do you want to feel? A stinging regret deep in your gut that you could've worked harder? Or a nervous peace?

In that moment, you want to feel that you gave it your all. You didn't burn yourself out in the process but you also didn't leave those grades to chance. You worked efficiently – not just harder but smarter. You can open those results knowing you did your best. That is enough.

When we talk about getting started, maybe results day is the place to begin. Rather than looking at the textbooks or piles of notes, think of the overarching goal and how you want to feel on that day. You will never be able to guarantee grades but you can guarantee how you approach them. You get to choose how hard you work and how to optimise your life to make learning feel fun. Results day is not a day at all. Results day is just a mindset and it starts now.

In these pages, we are going to focus on revision tactics to optimise your performance in our current school system but it is important to recognise that grades are not everything. It took me so long to realise that school isn't just a tick box: memorise a few pages, achieve a letter on a piece of paper and happily move on. School is a stepping stone in your journey to self-growth (deep, I know!). The more you learn, the greater your world perspective and the better equipped you are to tackle the challenges you'll face in the future. For example, when you develop your essay skills, it goes beyond getting that A*. It gives you the ability to craft good emails, express your thoughts and view the media with a critical eye, such as examining the connotations of words they choose in headlines. When you study languages, you can one day go to that country and impress the locals when you know the word for . . . recycling (because that's everyone's favourite conversation starter, thanks GCSE French!). School is just a stepping stone. Grades or not, it is a place for you to learn and grow. The whole idea of school is to shape you and challenge you so you become a person with well-informed and fully fledged opinions. Dealing with exam stress is preparing you for the intensity of real-life work. Studying in team settings is teaching you to be an effective leader and to cooperate with other personalities. There is so much to gain from school that goes beyond letters on a piece of paper and it took me entering the real world after sixth form to realise it. You see, you are only ever viewing life through the glasses of your own perspective, balanced on the tip of your nose and tinting the conclusions you draw. School gives you new lenses to see the world in all its wonder, colour and complexity. The more lenses you possess, the more opportunities you have to clarify your viewpoint and the more likely you are to change the world. I want to help you make the most of your learning opportunities so you can empower yourself to use this education for the better!

Before we break down the idea of motivation, I'm going to take you back to me as a 14-year-old student. What a crazy age that was. I was juggling family issues, extreme mid-puberty insecurity and the many dramas of social life. Namely, mean girls at school, the invisible popularity ladder, friendship groups and the increasing influence of social media, with its comparative nature.

Oh, and then there were GCSEs.

When teachers' salaries are indirectly tied to how well their students do, it is unsurprising that their pressure is shoved onto us. As the two years of GCSEs went on, I grew increasingly stressed about what felt like the be-all and end-all of my life. In the Easter holidays, I heard that friends had revised for eight hours straight, when I'd only done two. I came to associate time off studying with feeling guilty.

The two main issues you can have with schoolwork are that you either care too much or you care too little. If you're too invested, you border on perfectionism and attach your self-worth firmly to the grades you get. If you don't care, you struggle to motivate yourself to achieve your potential. Understanding yourself as a student is important so that you can take the best actions for you.

The former was my issue. As I went through the school system, I began to connect my sense of self to the grades I achieved. I became known for doing well. Let me tell you, there is nothing more crippling than a reputation, good or bad. With an expectation from peers, teachers and ultimately myself to achieve good grades, I lost the fun of learning. If I got a B and not an A, I was disheartened. I used to dread peers asking, 'How did you do on the test?'. What I dreaded even more was when they squealed, 'I scored higher than *Jade.*'

I beat myself up enough that I didn't need others doing it too.

Reputation can be seen as a compliment – in a way, it was nice that people expected me to do well. However, at the same time, the pressure that came with being a high achiever heightened my stress levels. At parents' evening, I would hear teachers say, 'Oh, of course she'll get an A*,' as though grades dropped in my lap without work. I felt added pressure from everyone around me that those grades needed to be easy.

Equally, if you have been saddled with a reputation of being 'average', it's like someone dropped you on the rung of a ladder and told you that you will never ascend. They tilt your head downwards and away from higher goals and tell you to be happy here because some rungs just aren't for you. We all make judgements about how teachers feel about us, and if you feel like a teacher has no hope for you to achieve higher, you may fall into the trap of giving up, or settling for lower than what you believe you're capable of. I like to think of reputations as glass ceilings. When the expectations are too high, revision is unhealthily driven by fear that one bad grade will cause the ceiling above you to crumble. If people's expectations are too low, the ceiling limits your potential like a cage. Expectations from both yourself and others carry a heaviness which can lead you to give up. It can be hard to stay motivated when you feel like it's you against the world.

The causes of a lack of academic motivation can be broken down to three main factors: lack of inspiration, conformity and circumstance. For example, you might be uninspired and distracted, influenced by your peers who hate school or so busy dealing with family issues that grades aren't a priority. All three are valid but you can still find a way to work with these factors and find some motivation.

LAZINESS

I like to call this a 'lack of inspiration'. Us teenagers get a bad rep for being 'lazy' and 'unmotivated' compared to other generations but I don't think this is our fault. We are in the age of distraction. We've been trained to tailor our lives to what we find immediately interesting. If we don't like something, we swipe. But when this translates to schoolwork, things get tough. Unfortunately, we can't just study the subjects we're interested in. There are other skills we have to learn, whether we like them or not. We don't absorb new concepts in six seconds. We can't swipe up when the test question gets hard.

It is this combination of shorter attention spans, a desire for entertainment and a love of answers over questions that makes us lazy. Why struggle through a maths question when I can watch Netflix?

And so I come back to the idea of 'lack of inspiration'. Clearly, in the dry way you've been introduced to that algebra problem, or told to memorise ten geography facts for next week, you've come to see learning as an avoidable chore, rather than something exciting. It is here we need to light that fire again.

You need to start seeing why this difficult subject is so incredible and loved (as hard as that might feel!). How those algebra problems are the basis of forecasting the weather or how that geography case study happened to real people on the other side of the world and you learning about is broadening your world perspective. These tasks are making you a better problem solver and solution finder.

At school, we are never encouraged to look beyond the spec or to watch extra YouTube videos on a subject simply because it is interesting. If you hate a subject, dare to ask yourself: why? Is it just hard and that makes you feel insecure? Do your friends not like it? Or is it just that you don't know how it could be interesting? If the latter, maybe it's up to you to inspire yourself. It is easy to find motivation when you see why learning something is valuable.

These are mental aspects of laziness, the barriers that stop you taking action. We'll be tackling the practical aspects of laziness and smashing procrastination with easily implementable systems as the book goes on.

CONFORMITY

Oh, this is a good one. We would never admit it, but half of what we like, what we do and what we believe is down to the people around us. If your mates wear a new style, you're more likely to wear it too. If your friendship group doesn't care about school . . . surprise! You probably won't care either.

The idea of conformity is simple. We subconsciously copy others to benefit ourselves. For example, we copy friends for social gain. Human beings want to be liked or accepted because we are social animals and this is beneficial to us.

We copy people in positions of authority because they have influence and/or are experts. We trust their opinions and systems because we believe they will benefit us. The list goes on. Conformity is not inherently bad. However, when conforming to social norms because you want to fit in with your peers conflicts with your personal goals, this is an issue. Why should you care less about school to be cooler? Do school and friendship need to be mutually exclusive? Does not talking to your friend for a whole lesson mean you won't still be good friends? Probably not. It just means you can focus better.

Sometimes you have to choose when to conform or not to optimise a certain benefit. It's okay if your friends have different goals. It says nothing about how well you get on with each other and I would never suggest cutting off friendship for the sake of school. But what I am saying is, ask yourself: do I downplay how much I care about grades to fit in with my friends? If you answered 'yes' then firstly you're a legend for admitting it. And secondly, ask yourself if Future You in five years would make the same choice.

You can pursue doing well at school *and* be cool *and* have a good social life. Remember that!

CIRCUMSTANCES

And lastly, quite possibly the most difficult source of demotivation to combat is your circumstances. Not everyone has flawless health, access to Nobel Prize winners for advice, and a private study space with a slide and ball pit. And even if you do (a ball pit? I'm jealous!), we all have issues. Being a student is so tough. Seriously. The academic system pretends that exams are our whole lives, ignoring the nuance of everything that makes us, us. Whatever elements of your life you're juggling, be it mental health struggles, supporting your family, caring for others, navigating social life, or just the existential crises of growing up, I want you to know that this book sees that. This book recognises you as a complex human. This book recognises that the grade you get will not show everything behind the scenes, and that a pass grade for one person will merit the same congratulations of top grades for another. This book is an invitation to motivate yourself from within, taking into account everything else in your life. We all deserve to enter these exams with sharp pens blazing and brains bulging. Because at the end of the day, the details of your circumstances weren't your choice. But the choice you *do* have is how you react to it. You've got this.

Now that we've considered why you might not be motivated, let's think about how to light that fire. It's not that you wake up one day, see a bright light with a grade in it and suddenly you're set for the rest of the year. Motivation either comes from intrinsic or extrinsic sources. Intrinsic motivation stems from a love of learning and the process itself. It's about finding enough joy in the act of studying that you don't mind spending another hour on it. It's being so fascinated by what you're studying that you're eager to learn more. It's looking forward to the feeling of entering an exam and knowing the answer to a question, or making yourself a vibey study playlist of low-fi beats and looking forward to the cosy songs. Sometimes, I was motivated by how the topic we were learning in class was really cool and could be applied to other aspects of life. I loved how learning about plant cells in biology made me look at my houseplants in a whole new way, or how my business GCSE class helped me better understand my mum's job. Even though I didn't enjoy reviewing it, I loved that learning made me feel more informed on something useful. But sometimes it is the extrinsic sources of motivation that pull us along in the short term. These are external rewards, such as the grades themselves, verbal praise from parents, or winning a bet if you get a certain percentage. Extrinsic motivation is guided by outcomes. You don't need to care about learning as long as you get the result you want. Extrinsic motivation starts with identifying your long-term sources of motivation, such as a job or university, and understanding that all the effort you invest now will pay off for Future You. Both forms of motivation are useful, but intrinsic motivation is usually more sustainable. If you can find a way to make the process more enjoyable, as opposed to only looking at the outcome, you will likely put more time and effort in, resulting in good grades anyway.

Simon Sinek, an author and motivational speaker who wrote an influential book called *Start with Why*, once did a TED talk about the success of the company Apple. He broke down how we view the external world and the stories we tell ourselves in setting goals. He concluded that it's not about the *what*, nor the *how* in goal-setting – it's about the *why*. Not what grade you want to get or how you're going to achieve it, but WHY you want to push for it. Maybe you love learning and the pursuit of better grades is part of a deeper pursuit of knowledge. Maybe you want to prove something to yourself or your family. To say, 'Look, I struggled. And I still achieved this insane thing I'm proud of.' Or perhaps you have a dream university or career in mind. Even if you don't know the specifics of what you want to do (I don't!), we all know that better grades give us more options in life. Grades aren't everything, but they do help! Rather than motivating yourself around achieving a specific letter, focus on your larger *why* and whatever you need to fulfil it.

Your *why* should be long-term. I like to think of goal-setting as two-tiered. First, define the high-level long-term goal. Then follow with smaller, more manageable blocks that serve that higher purpose. Here is an example of my 'why'. I put it on a Post-it note on my wall during my GCSEs:

> *I am worthy of being successful at school because I want to **prove** to myself that I can achieve the grades I want, especially when I'm struggling.*

Knowing why you try will keep you going in your last hour of revision and motivate you to seek help when necessary. What is your why? Motivation is a *feeling* and thus not a reliable reason to study every day. Get clear on your why, and channel it to set up systems and habits which keep you going even when the feeling fades.

FIXED VS GROWTH MINDSET

A lot of research has been done on working out what makes the most successful students succeed. Interestingly, it is not natural intelligence or IQ. It is mindset and consistency. Perhaps the biggest takeaway in this whole section is that *you* define your work ethic.

A fixed mindset is the belief that you are not naturally suited to something. For example, you're struggling with a maths problem and you say, 'I hate maths. I suck at it. I always have and I always will.' But the second you attribute your performance to some innate ability (or lack of it), all room for improvement disappears. You curse yourself to this fixed place.

A growth mindset on the other hand is the recognition that you will struggle and get things wrong but you can always learn and do better. In the earlier example, instead of giving up and attributing the struggle to their bad maths skills, someone with a growth mindset would take on the challenge and push harder, perhaps by looking up videos of similar problems or asking a friend for help. It is a belief that you're not there . . . *yet*. But you will be. The power of the word 'yet' is enough to transform grades, how you feel about rejection and even life paths.

I don't understand this maths problem *yet*. But I can and I will.

I am not good at chemistry *yet*. But with enough work, I can be and I will be.

I don't like English language *yet*. But I can find a reason to make it interesting.

This mindset changed my academic life. I'd always catch myself moaning about how bad I was at subjects without really giving myself a chance to get better. If I believed there was no hope for me, how could I ever motivate myself to improve?

During A levels, I embraced the opportunity to get better. It inspired me to view failure more constructively and actively seek out my teachers for support. I even set up a weekly 'check-in' with my maths teacher to go over questions I got wrong that week. It's more effort, sure. But the other option is sucking forever because you choose to. And that's a waste of all your potential.

Even the great Albert Einstein said, 'It's not that I'm so smart, it's just that I stay with problems longer.'

If you don't get something straight away – amazing, you're human. But all you need to do to be the next Albert Einstein is believe you'll get there eventually and have the grit to keep trying.

To round this chapter off, think about this: motivation is not a gift from the gods that blesses just a lucky few of us, nor is it a one-time thing that you achieve once and have forever. Motivation is a daily choice, one helped by changing your mindset, recognising what is holding you back and then putting systems in place that help you stay disciplined when motivation fades.

So remind me, why do you want to succeed again?

You remember?

Okay, then it's time to start!

PUT IT IN PRACTICE:

- What is your reason for feeling unmotivated? (Lack of inspiration, conformity or circumstance?)
- Write down your *why*. Think about your intrinsic motivations and long-term extrinsic motivations. Put a note about them somewhere visible in your room.
- What do you normally tell yourself when you are struggling with something? Do you have a fixed mindset of thinking you are not naturally good at it? How can you make yourself believe that you're not there *yet* . . . but that you can be with more effort?

From now on, every chapter will end with a short section from a student who recently went through the education system. Many of these authors are StudyTubers who are well known online for giving academic advice. We all learn differently, so it is important that this book encompasses a range of perspectives! If you're not already feeling motivated, just wait. Every page from here on out is infused with luck and good energy. You're welcome.

CHAPTER 2

THE ACADEMIC SYSTEM

Before we get stuck into how to study and smash your exams, welcome to the most serious chapter of the lot. I want to give you something that I never had during my GCSEs: perspective.

When you're in the pressured bubble of the education system, you never take a step back and realise that it is just that: a system. Everything from the exam boards to the long days of school, to cramming for exams and memorising information – it's all an intricate web that goes beyond just you. The idea that exams are the best way to test young people is not fact, it is a decision that has been made. The existence of school rankings, memory-based questions and employing a standard metric to measure the answers is a choice. Now that I have finished my exams, I see the system for the first time. I see its purposes, its merits and, most importantly, its flaws.

You do not have a choice in how you are tested. Whether the exams suit your style of learning or not, you will have to take them. What you do have a choice in is how you approach the system. How you use it to truly learn and how you can optimise the style of testing to give yourself the most options in life.

Understanding what you're facing gives you the space to breathe and remind yourself that you have merit beyond the grade you are given. If you've ever wondered why the education system feels so stressful, I hope this chapter will show you that it's completely natural to feel that way. This is a reminder that though we must slay the exams to give ourselves options, we can meaningfully critique our system in a way which is empowering. We can see school as a game – and one which we are going to win.

Welcome to a (very brief!) history of the academic system, your place in it and what you can take away from it.

A RAPID-FIRE HISTORY OF THE ENGLISH EDUCATION SYSTEM (OR: WHY IT'S NOT WEIRD TO FEEL STRESSED)

Every day when I went to school, I assumed that everything I was learning had been meaningfully designed for the benefit of every student's unique needs. I assumed that every test question had been carefully considered to give us all the best footing in life and to test all types of intelligence. Surely that's the job of the people in power, right?: to ensure the next generation learns about themselves and the world in a way that empowers them to shape it. I imagined that modern-day schooling was founded on the notion of wanting the best for each individual so they could carve out the life of their dreams.

Ha! I wish.

While this is undoubtedly true for many of our incredible teachers who pour their hearts and souls into our education (we love you!), the system needs work. One day, I was listening to 'Akimbo', one of my favourite podcasts by popular teacher, economist and marketing guru Seth Godin. In it, he dissected the history of the education system in the US and how its origins underscore many of the flaws in today's system, which fails to empower students to love learning. At its core, the education system went mainstream not because the government decided everyone deserved to learn, but indirectly for profit. Public education came with industrialisation, which began at the end of the 1700s in the UK and saw people move away from agricultural work to spend long days in the new factories, often in unfavourable conditions. It was not surprising that some of these workers rebelled, rejecting the strict rules of the factory system that emphasised productivity over human rights – I mean, who wants to sit in one place all day and just do as they're told? Workers' lack of obedience was not ideal for production and it was clear to the factory owners and ruling classes that a new system was needed to train future workers to better abide by rules and learn discipline. Enter the education system.

Designed not around personal growth, critical thinking or enhancing one's world perspective, the first iterations of mainstream education for the masses were built around encouraging obedience, collective learning and rote memorisation which could be applied to labour. Older and more able pupils were taught with standardised repetitive exercises (did someone say 'reciting definitions'?). Schooling had a factory-like feel, with the batch production of students based on age group rather than ability or passions, specific metrics to define 'good' and power dynamics that stripped divergent thinking. School was not training you to ask good questions, but rather answer the ones they wanted.

Exams were introduced to suitably reassure outsiders that pupils were prepared for careers in the ever-growing administration and service industries. It was helpful to train students to memorise specific facts word-for-word. It was less useful for students to develop critical thinking, a tool which could be used to question the people at the top of the system.

Though there have been many shifts in the academic system from that time, such as the introduction of a wide range of subjects, we still employ a lot of the same methods of learning. We are all familiar with the passive absorbing of carefully curated knowledge.

I studied French for five years at school. I learned about the past tense, the present tense, the pluperfect; I even memorised a few passages and recited them in writing exams. But the obsession with *theory* instead of practice meant I came out of Year 11 not even close to fluent. That's the thing: learning *about* something is not the same as learning something. In my gap year, I spent a month on an intensive language course in France. I lived with an amazing 60-year-old French woman in a stereotypically French apartment in Montpellier. Through fumbling over words like a babbling baby, I came out of France actually able to hold a conversation. I was both amazed and suddenly disheartened; something about those five years learning French needed revision.

Equally I have friends who had no interest in reading long books, but could run like Usain Bolt or sew a dress from scratch in days. With increasingly more theory added to practical subjects and a reduction in coursework, my friends weren't able to excel in the subjects most important to them or, worse still, were made to think that they were less valuable than the core academic subjects.

The rote way we learn in school today was designed for an old world – the economic imperative of that time. Nowadays, the world is changing so quickly. Why isn't our education system changing equally as quickly to prepare us?

So, everything you've ever learned was apparently only for an exam but that still doesn't explain why it feels so stressful. At school, I remember thinking I was weak and incapable of handling large workloads. I assumed the system itself had to be optimal and fair, so if I struggled, it was all on me.

Spoiler: learning should not feel stressful. It's not just you. It's a system of stress.

The system is deeply flawed and the focus on ranking is often at the expense of what the school, its teachers and its pupils really need to thrive. Not everything can be measured by an exam or an Ofsted ranking. But sadly, to compare schools in the current system, it's been determined that you need a standardised metric. Welcome to standardised exams.

I actually think the concept of exams is okay. Being tested is a great tool for learning. Exams, in isolation, are awesome. They show you where you're at with your abilities and tell you where you need to improve. Exams are not inherently stressful because pieces of paper are not stressful. What *is* stressful is the context of the system around it. By every standard of the school, performance needs to improve. The government has chosen the way in which they want this assessed – annual exams – and our beloved teachers are the driving force of getting students to perform. Even when teachers buffer the pressure from schools, we still feel it.

The way we are scored to a standard involves what Dr Frances Maratos, a professor of emotion science, calls 'insecure competition'. If we really, really wanted you as an individual to succeed, we would rank you against your own performance and progress. Instead, you are always ranked against others. Competition is not just with yourself and your abilities but with grade boundaries, peers and other schools. There are known negative repercussions to not getting the grade you want, like not being able to advance to the next level of studies or get the job you want. This is the issue with a standardised way of learning and grading – having to focus on a percentage score and test of memory kills the root of learning: curiosity. It's why we often stop loving learning.

When your results are tied to the performance of institutions, it's no surprise there are expectations placed on you. As someone who adores learning and how it enriches my world perspective, I really think that the fundamental system to support learning just needs a little work. A system that *needs* you to succeed for rankings on a wall is still, in my opinion, not a healthy system.

The world school comes from the Greek word σχολή, which first meant leisure or free time. Ancient Greek philosophers believed that for true learning to occur, students needed to be given space and time to ponder ideas, exchange thoughts and sit with problems. If you don't understand something straight away, that shouldn't be frowned upon. You just probably haven't spent enough time turning over the problem or discussing it with friends. Without expectations to memorise a concept for a grade, you're incentivised to understand the concept for fun and even apply it to your own life.

As a student doing my GCSEs, I didn't question the bigger picture, or wonder how it came to be like this. I woke up each day, dragged myself from bed to bus stop, brain half in social media. I went to each class, I didn't think about why I was learning what I was learning, I didn't wonder why teachers put so much pressure on us to perform or why every lesson from Year 9 onwards mentioned exams. I didn't consider that there are other ways to value a person beyond mark schemes created by exam boards and I definitely didn't realise that the school was just as scared as I was for results day.

If you've never learned about the wider academic system, I hope this has empowered you to see stress as a product of a system that loves competition. Knowing this, you can take education into your own hands, see it as a game you can play and take the expectations placed on you lightly. It's not personal.

STANDARDISED METRICS

Why aren't we measured on how fast we run? What kind of friend we are? How funny we are? How good we are at public speaking? How well we can knit?

As Einstein says, 'If you judge a fish by its ability to climb a tree, it will live its whole life believing that it is stupid.'

I do believe that every single person is flexible and capable of learning whatever they want but it is useful to consider that certain methods of assessment suit certain people's skillsets more than others. For example, a system of theoretical exams with increasingly less coursework is best for people who can condense two or three years of study into one day of blurting down knowledge. How niche. However, this standard does not of course reflect your holistic potential. You have many and varied skills, talents and merits, and they are not all represented by how well you can recite some text or find the value of 'x' under time-pressured conditions.

The current education system does not value practical subjects in the same way it does academic ones, which is evident in the increase of theory-based grading. If you are less academic, it's unsurprising you hate school because it's hard to view your talents with the same value as those that are eagerly celebrated every day.

But that is the system as it stands. So what can we do? Well, one good thing about such a standardised method of testing is that you can learn the system like a game. The more rigid it is, the easier it is to understand and optimise for. This knowledge is empowering. So, let's work out how to smash the given standard, even while we remember that it is not all there is. If the system wants to give you stress, we're going to throw mindfulness and evidence-based revision techniques back at them like highlighted artillery. Over the next few chapters, we are going to dig into the depths of how to succeed.

If you're not thrilled by the thought of exams, you don't have to lie and say you love them. Instead, notice how you do feel towards them. Do you feel angry? Great. Because you can decide from here on out that you're going to channel that anger into efficiency – to beat the exam boards at their own game. Do you feel unmotivated because exams don't suit you? Understandable and valid. Recognise that you have incredible talents beyond the system and that learning to get through exams in the easiest way possible is a gift to your future self. Do you feel scared? Awesome, I did too. Fear is so natural in the lead up to exams because it comes from uncertainty. You'll never know all the questions you'll be asked but you *can* become fluent in the exotic tongue of exam technique. This book is going to prep you for those exams until you're strutting into the hall like you invented GCSEs.

SO, WHY TRY?

The system isn't perfect. You can probably see that now. The reasons we get stressed are not because we're weak or incapable (how dare they!) but because the system is designed for us to compete around standards that may not suit every learner.

But if you know the system is flawed, why motivate yourself to learn?

There are so many reasons why it's important to take learning into your own hands as a teenager. Here are my top five reasons why I worked hard (bloody hard!) to achieve what I did at GCSE and A level – and why you should too.

SCHOOL IS WHAT YOU MAKE OF IT

The more you put in, the more you get out. One of the most empowering parts of the academic system is knowing that you can control how you approach it. You can experiment and test out study routines without having to worry about not being paid by an employer. If you get it wrong to start with, no one is going to fire you, you can just have another go.

You also have time to ask questions and get curious beyond the textbook. You can use the syllabus as a starting point to find subjects you're passionate about. As a teenager, your sole, full-time job is studying. Or, put another way, your whole job is learning about the world through the frameworks given to you. Seize it, go beyond, learn more and motivate yourself to see how special this time of your life is. Whenever I speak to adults, they wish they had more free time to just . . . learn.

Top tip: go and watch TED talks related to the class topics and discuss them with your friends. Explore YouTube videos and podcasts to learn about alternative opinions to what you're being taught. What you're taught in the specification is an incredible taster of everything that subject has to offer! If you find something interesting, I dare you to go beyond. Even if extra reading doesn't instantly get you a better grade, it comes back to the idea of intrinsic motivation discussed in chapter 1. The more you find joy in the *process* of learning, and the more you can view it as useful to your own interests, the more likely you are to organically succeed!

OPTIONS

At the end of the day grades just give you options. If you have no idea what you want to do with your life, trying hard at school is one way to broaden your horizons. The universities you can apply to, the subjects you can study, the job you can get – all of it is indirectly impacted by that sheet of paper at the end of exams. It is a radical act of self-love and self-compassion to care about your education because everything you learn will indirectly help Future You.

DISCIPLINE AND HARD WORK

Ah yes, if this isn't the older generations' favourite. Dare I say it, though: they have a point. Hard work is, as the name suggests, hard. But I learned so many incredible habits in my secondary school life. I taught myself how to adopt a routine and stick to it. I learned how to set a goal and do everything possible to achieve it. For example, I believed wholeheartedly that I could and would achieve an A* in A level chemistry if I worked hard, and smart, enough. If I created the right action plan, optimised my teachers and resources, I was capable of success. In my life beyond school, this mindset has proven invaluable. When it came to creating business projects, working in internships or writing university assignments, I had already learned how to create ambitious goals and work for them. The world is so full of opportunity if you choose to see it that way.

The world also has pressing, complex problems that require a hard-working mindset. If you can teach yourself how to solve academic problems you don't enjoy, you'll be better equipped to tackle all the unpleasant problems in your later life. You are a tiny agent in a massive system but you have so much power to create change. Learning to strive for big goals through over-coming smaller problems will equip you to view the world as malleable.

THE REINFORCING FEEDBACK LOOP OF SUCCESS

According to positive psychology, success breeds success, which breeds more success. School is an opportunity for you to **define what success means to you** and optimise for it. What are you telling yourself? Are you the 'student who scraped a pass' or the 'student who smashed a pass and is capable of achieving whatever they want in life'? You passed *and* you are one step closer to a lifetime of your chosen success. For me, working hard to achieve the GCSEs I wanted was such a confidence boost. It was a reminder that anything I wanted to do in life was within reach if only I developed the right strategies. Feeling successful makes you reach for further success, however you define it.

THE ACADEMIC SYSTEM IS A GAME, AND YOU CAME TO WIN

As I have already mentioned, the system is not designed for each individual person; instead, it's a very specific game with very specific rules, and therefore you can find a formula to win. Thinking of exams as a game you play against an arbitrary system takes the pressure out of them. Whether the style of the academic system suits you or not, you can learn how to strategise to get the best out of it. Later life is going to be full of other systems you have to navigate and some of those will suit you and some won't. If you can learn how to beat this system as a teenager then you'll be well prepared for other challenges in life.

You're not weird for feeling stressed by all the hoops of exams and coursework and constant assessment you have to jump through. There's a long way to go to developing student-specific growth, learning and critical thinking without the terrifying pressure associated with exam grades. But for now, this is where we are. The game will teach you so many life lessons, if only you choose to play – and win.

ADVICE FROM . . . VIOLA HELEN

If you had asked me at 16 where I saw myself at 24, I would probably have told you that I would be a graduate from a top university, living in central London, with a fancy corporate job. The reality? Far from it. I would never have believed you if you told me that, despite taking a gap year both before and after university to travel, after graduating from the University of Oxford, I would spontaneously move to Portugal entirely by myself. That I would consciously choose to move to a country where I did not know the language, where I did not have a job lined up, and where I did not know anyone . . . But I did.

Travelling around the world and living abroad has altered my perspective on the education system. In the UK, there is incredible pressure to excel academically because society constantly emphasises that good grades = getting into a good university = getting a better, higher-paid job. I will not deny that having a strong academic background is certainly beneficial and will open doors to many opportunities. However, with this academic pressure, there is also a huge rush to find a job straight out of university and to work your way up the corporate ladder as soon as possible in order to seem 'successful'. Societal expectations give students no room to even question whether they actually want to do the jobs they are so desperately applying for.

And what is the rush? I have slowly realised that we are going to be working for the next 40 years of our lives; surely we are allowed to take some time to learn, grow and develop before plunging headfirst into a job we do not even want. Whilst this may very well be easy for me to say as an Oxford graduate, I promise you that there is so much more to life than attaining top grades in order to get a particular type of job. Though we should certainly work as hard as we can whilst at school (because being academically strong provides a safety net when entering the real world), we should not forget that grades do not define us and do not dictate our future. There are numerous jobs and professions out there requiring skills which can be learnt independently from traditional education settings and through real-life experiences.

Here in Portugal, I do not feel the same pressure to have my life 'figured out' by x age. I am currently open to everything life has to offer: I am taking time to develop the skills I am interested in; I am dedicating time to learning Portuguese; and I am exploring various different career options through networking and speaking to professionals. I am learning, exploring and evolving, and, despite feeling extremely conflicted about going against societal expectations, I know that this is the right decision for me. Remember, there is more to life than the academic system. While you're in it, the best thing you can do is your utmost best. It's enough.

CHAPTER 3

HOW WE LEARN

I can definitely say that the first time an end of chapter test was slapped on my desk in Year 7, I had never thought about how we actually learned. Information would pass from textbook to class notes, to my lazy eyes as I reread everything and hoped it would magically go in so I could pass my tests. I heard myths that if I slept with a textbook under my pillow, I would wake up a genius. I heard that if I listened to Spanish audio recordings every night, I would wake up fluent (I wish!). Revision was a fingers-crossed guessing game.

It wasn't until I dug into the basics of human memory that I began to understand how we can optimise revision. Rather than spending more hours at the desk, I needed to change the techniques I was using to begin with. Rather than working harder at every study session, I needed to be strategic about *when* I was revising and how often.

My long study sessions were made miserable by their lack of success in tests. I needed to transform my revision into something more effective.

HOW DO WE ACTUALLY LEARN?

From reading into evidence-based revision techniques, I created a handy framework called SAAD (pronounced 'saaah-d' like you're prolonging the *a* in sad until you're happy), where each letter stands for a way to make my learning more successful based on science. Now every time I come to study, I mentally go through the SAAD checklist and ask myself if what I am doing fulfils these requirements. This framework is a way to make sure your revision works. Everything I'm about to share with you is an easily digestible version of scientifically backed studies about human cognition.* This chapter will cover the science behind learning, dubbed the 'principles of learning', and position them in the context of different revision techniques you're familiar with. It will equip you with a simple framework to judge every piece of revision you do from here on out and this knowledge completely changed my revision life. If you remember one thing from this book, make it this framework. Get ready.

You're going to come out of this chapter turning miserable and sad revision into time-effective SAAD revision, which really works.

SAAD: Spaced repetition

So there's a guy called Hermann Ebbinghaus. A pretty cool guy. Some call him the Father of Memory because he was the first person to carry out experiments about human retention. He sat in a room alone and forced himself to memorise thousands of nonsense words, measuring his ability to recall these words over time. As I said, a cool guy (with lots of free time . . .). He discovered the Forgetting Curve, which paved

---

* If you'd like to read more on this, I've listed the full studies on the Bibliography page at the end of the book.

the way for how we think about memory retention. The graph is shown below:

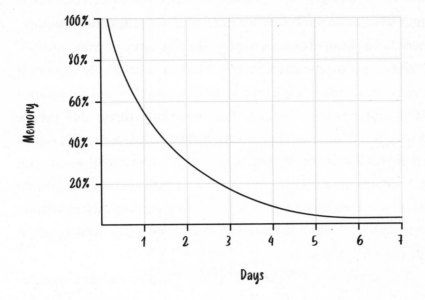

THE FORGETTING CURVE

As you can see, your memory starts strong. You revise a concept, you understand it and you can readily recall the information. For example, I tell you the name of my dog, Willow. It's right there in your mind as you tell her to 'sit' and 'fetch'. You shake Willow's paw and decide she is, in fact, very cute. But memory decays exponentially. Over just seven days of not revising it, you can't recall the concept anymore. You come back to see my dog and you just can't remember her name. You desperately ask her to fetch a half-chewed toy and she stares at you blankly. Who, me?

This is actually quite sad. I can vividly remember getting the odd burst of motivation to spend the day revising. I would get all my notes, feel like a Revision Queen for putting in the hours and leave my session confident in my knowledge. But that session would be a one-off, I didn't have the systems in place to review those concepts again later in the week. Before I knew it, that day spent revising was for nothing: I forgot almost all of it after two weeks.

So how can you improve this curve? We don't want to learn something and watch our knowledge slip away faster than students leaving school when the bell rings. Thankfully, there is a solution. Maybe you've heard of 'spaced repetition'. It's a bit of a buzzword in the world of productivity social media. I was first introduced to it by my good friend and YouTuber Ali Abdaal. The idea is that you review information again, multiple times, at set intervals from first learning it. Have a look at the new graph below:

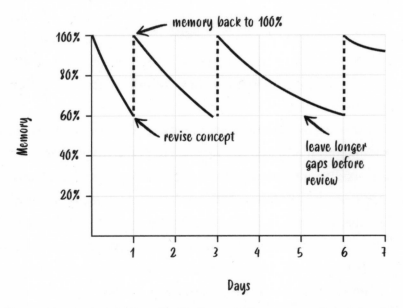

Every time you review the information, you reset your memory back to 100 per cent. The idea is that you catch your memory just as you're about to forget what you learned.

The beauty of spaced repetition is that the more you review a concept, the longer the gap you can leave before reviewing it again. Eventually, the information becomes so ingrained in your long-term memory that you can review it once a month, or once every few months.

The secret is not cramming for ten hours once in a while. It's not about working harder at all. It's about working smarter, for less time, but consistently. Reviewing concepts for five minutes every day with spaced repetition is the scientifically backed secret to good grades.

There are different ways to create systems of accountability for spaced repetition. For example, you can create a spreadsheet with all your topics and input the date of when you last studied it. You can then calculate the next best time for review based on the forgetting curve, such as going over your flashcards tomorrow, in three days and then after a week. In the next chapter, I will also discuss flashcard apps which have inbuilt spaced repetition functions to help you optimise human learning.

However you end up revising, you need to use spaced repetition. It's not about revising for longer, just more frequently.

Welcome to your first snippet of understanding how you learn!

Spaced repetition is the first step in turning sad revision to SAAD revision.

S<u>A</u>AD: Active recall

Right, friends, let's go on another deep dive.

There's another interesting guy called Stephen Kosslyn, a prominent psychologist and neuroscientist. He split up human learning into two overarching maxims: 'Think it Through' and

'Make and Use Associations'. Both of these maxims capture principles of the science of learning that explain why certain revision techniques do (and don't!) work.

So what does it mean to Think It Through?

The idea is that the more you are forced to think deeply about an idea, the more you remember it. Turning over a concept in your head strengthens the synaptic connections in your brain, which are the gaps between neurons and allow the transfer of information in the brain. Continuously revisiting thoughts strengthens the neural pathways to accessing that information, just like being forced to recall facts is more beneficial than passively reading them on a page.

The principle of Think It Through leads us to the A in SAAD revision: active recall.

We don't like to think. Even when we revise, we would prefer to reread our notes, highlight words in a textbook or annotate text rather than stare at a blank page and recite our existing knowledge.

We look for shortcuts.

To this day, even though I understand the power of active testing, I find myself rereading articles and books rather than forcing myself to see what I can recall first.

Without actively recalling information, you don't actually know what you don't know.

Imagine you're reading a textbook. There is a fully labelled diagram in front of you. Definitions are neatly explained on the page. You even have step-by-step explanations of scientific processes or historical events. Everything you are reading makes sense. But if you understand the information and find yourself nodding along, you are lulling yourself into believing you *know* the information, which is not the same as simply understanding it. If you've ever done a biology exam, you'll know that it is one thing to confidently understand a biological process but another to recall every step, with every keyword, without a single prompt. And this is exactly what the mark scheme requires of you.

When you are passive, it is easy, but you reveal nothing to yourself. When you are active, it is uncomfortable, challenging and requires mental effort. Which is why it is the most effective use of your time.

Let's look at an example of two sets of flashcards. The first one has a labelled diagram of a plant cell. You look over the diagram and check if you know the details.

Cell wall? Yep. Makes sense. Looks like a wall.

Nucleus? Of course. Easy. A black dot.

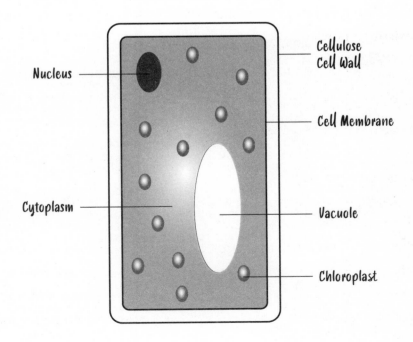

Now here is more of an active recall diagram:

What type of cell is this?

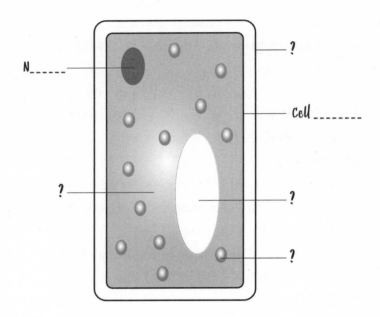

N_ _ _ _ _ _

?

Cell _ _ _ _ _ _ _ _

?

?

?

What is the cell wall made out of?

Suddenly, with hardly any prompts, your brain has to actively recall the labels of the diagram. This truly tests whether or not you know them. The mini questions force you to recall your knowledge and engage with the flashcard. You can put the answers on the back or double check your notes to see if you were right!

Active recall goes against human nature, as we always want to find the path of least resistance with revision. Remember, the harder the revision feels, the more effective it probably is. Get that brain working.

Before we move on, a quick question for you.

Can you remember what the S stands for in SAAD revision? Have a think.

Two words. One beginning with S. The other with R.

Can you see why me asking is demonstrating your use of this principle? If you can't remember, flick back now! I'll be asking you again soon.

SA<u>A</u>D: Associations

The second of Kosslyn's maxims, that he calls 'Make and Use Associations', fits into active recall but deserves its own mention. Why is this important?

Information does not sit in your brain in isolation. You don't have a section of the brain reserved for historical dates, a part for maths equations or a bunch of neurons labelled 'inorganic chemistry'. Instead, everything you've ever learned is inter-twined. One big ingenious mess of knowledge. Some people think that learning something distinctly different from what you already know will save you getting confused when in reality, a powerful principle of revision techniques is *connecting* what you're learning to existing knowledge. Making associations and using them.

I'm going to demonstrate this in the Least Professional Revision Way.

You've been invited as a plus-one to a party. Drink in hand, you go over to meet the host. You smile at them, introduce yourself, shake their hand and then get ready to ask the make-or-break question: 'What's your name?'

But you're immediately mentally cursing yourself because the second you ask this, you've entered an invisible contract to try your very best to remember that person's name, whether it's common or completely new to you.

But you're horrible at remembering names.

You can already feel yourself repeating it in your head. *Charlotte. Charlotte. Charlotte. Charlotte. Charlotte. Charlotte. How hard can it be to remember the name Charlotte?*

Before you know it, you're enjoying the social event and no longer engaging in your mental relay of their name. You're swayed into the crowds with new names to recall and new conversations to fill your mind.

The party ends. You call out to thank the host and . . .

You can't remember her name for the life of you. Was it Catherine? Or Lucy? She looks like a Lucy but you're sure it started with a C. And then you're fumbling awkwardly, aware that she just let you into her house and you didn't even have the decency to remember her name.

If you had applied the second A in SAAD revision, you wouldn't have this issue.

Let's reverse. This girl reveals her name is Charlotte. You have a couple of seconds in your mind to think about what this name means to you. Do you know any Charlottes? Is there a celebrity with this name? If so, you must find a way to connect this new person with your existing idea of the name. For example, imagine your neighbour Charlotte's face on top of the face of this girl you just met. Make yourself think about the fact that the Charlotte who lives next door has different coloured hair to this new Charlotte. Maybe you're thinking of the British royal princess Charlotte, and that though this new woman is not a royal princess, you notice she carries herself with elegance. Or that she has a good enough vocabulary to remind you of famous author Charlotte Brontë. Whatever it is, make an association. It sounds silly but you are training your brain in those two seconds to create a rich retrieval cue to this person's name. You are giving them a space in your head by attaching them to your existing knowledge.

At the end of the party, you go to thank the host. Her name doesn't come to you immediately, but all of a sudden you're thinking about how she doesn't look like a royal princess or that her hair colour is different to your neighbour. The name returns to you. The association was a success. Social awkwardness helpfully avoided.

But what if her name wasn't Charlotte but one you've never heard before? Suddenly you're panicked that there are no existing associations to the name; there is no hope your memory will succeed. But the magic of associations is that they can be creative and unique to you.

I'll share with you a story of a girl I met at university. She is from Kosovo and has a beautiful name that I struggled *so hard* to remember. My fault, not hers.

Ujeza. Pronounced *oo-yay-zah.*

I don't know about you, but I don't know many Ujezas. I saw her every day in the hallway and, no matter what, couldn't link her name to anything I could remember.

Which is why you need to create your own associations. In my head, I broke her name down into the words *you, yay* and *star.*

I played a ten-second mental game with myself where I imagined this girl pointing at me, saying 'you', cheering 'yay' and then calling me a 'star' (quite an ego boost, I know). This vision of her pointing, cheering and saying 'star' allowed me to remember the sequence *you-yay-star,* which was enough to jog my memory of her name *oo-yay-zah.* Ujeza.

And now her name is easy.

What does this tangent show you?

Though this example isn't rooted in studying for an exam, it proves that memory requires a base. You can't expect to learn a brand new concept with no foundational knowledge to root it. 'Foundational material' is actually the backbone of additional information because it allows you to have an organised mental structure over time.

But how do you apply this to revision?

Let's take a historical fact you need to learn for a test about the Second World War. You need to remember key dates in a time-line but the long list of numbers and months in front of you feels completely overwhelming.

For example, the Second World War began on 1 September 1939. How can you remember this? Start thinking about what this day in September means to you. It can be anything. Is it usually cold in your country? Are the leaves starting to fall in autumn? I associate 1 September with the start of the academic year at school. Whatever it is, find a way to link this to the idea of the Second World War. Imagine autumn leaves falling when people heard the news or kids on their way to school. This mental image that you naturally associate with the date will help jog your memory in an intuitive way.

To remember the year 1939, look for any association you have to this number. Do you know anyone who is 39 years old? Do you deeply know any key dates in history around this time that will allow you to connect the start of the Second World War to this other event? Can you notice that 1939 has two 9s in it, which could represent *TWO* world wars? Whatever silly association you make, it will turn facts into a long-term element of memory through linking to what you definitely do know.

If you can find a way to make your revision connected, meaningful and built upon past knowledge, you will create rich retrieval cues to prompt you. And this is where long-term knowledge starts.

So, to recap, our sad revision is starting to look a bit more **S**paced, **A**ctive and **A**ssociated, hey? We're getting there.

SAAD: Desirable difficulty

As mentioned earlier, we love to go for shortcuts. We love to feel like we're doing hard work without actually thinking too hard. Which is why we need to check that our revision is desirably difficult.

If you hate a subject, you probably just find it hard.

Flashback to A Level chemistry again. Oof. I was not a fan of drawing molecules and reciting lab practicals. It was hard and, hence, not fun. At least, for a long time.

But you know what was fun? Reviewing English literature notes. I found it interesting and easy to process, so I would find myself revising it more than I needed to because it made me feel productive without much commitment.

Meanwhile, I would put off chemistry work. Rather than attacking it head on, I would hide from it and move the undone practice papers through my to-do lists like I was shuffling cards.

Desirable difficulty is about realising when something is hard and choosing to do it anyway. The last thing we want to do is torture ourselves in our free time with subjects we find hard but half the pain of revision is in choosing to start. SAAD revision asks you to know your academic pain points and, rather than ignoring them, *attack* them. With bows and arrows and guns and flamethrowers and an army of flashcards. This is how you will grow.

However, desirable difficulty is not just about choosing to revise the hard subjects but asking yourself during your revision if you're actually having to think. More than simply doing active recall, question how hard you're finding it. If it's easy, amazing! Do the harder stuff. Maybe you're ready to try a past paper, apply your knowledge to practice questions or to explain these concepts to a friend.

Invite yourself to seek the challenge. Getting better is not about repeating what you confidently know.

PUT IT IN PRACTICE:

So there you have it: here are four ways to really connect with the way we learn and that we can use every time we revise. Are we doing sad, unhelpful revision or are we doing SAAD revision?

S: Are you repeating this revision activity at spaced intervals? Or is this a one-off?

A: Are you revising actively? Are you thinking? Or are you just reading?

A: Are you associating this new information to knowledge you already have? How can you make links?

D: Is this activity desirably difficult? Can you make it more challenging, if necessary?

ADVICE FROM . . . ALI ABDAAL

After studying Medicine at University of Cambridge, Ali is both a junior doctor and YouTuber discussing all things productivity, studying, tech and living a happy life. He is also the king of study tips, so listen up!

I really struggled through my first year of medical school. I was taking copious notes, highlighting my lecture notes, and spending hours reading my textbooks. I'd feel like I understood something, but within a few days, I'd forget everything and have to start from scratch.

Then, in my second year, I discovered the world of evidence-based study techniques. Turns out researchers have been studying this for decades, with hundreds of experiments done on (mostly) students to figure out what strategies work best for understanding and remembering.

One of the most mind-blowing insights was that learning stuff isn't about putting things into our brain. It's about getting stuff out of our brain. In other words, rereading and summarising information in an attempt to force it into our brain isn't going to work. Instead, if we read it once and then test ourselves repeatedly, we're more likely to remember. It's the act of retrieving information from our brain that strengthens the connection to it.

When I discovered this, I reoriented my study and revision strategies around testing myself. The more I tested myself, the more I remembered. It also made studying much more fun – I made a spreadsheet with a list of topics, and I'd colour them in red, yellow and green, depending on how well I knew the topic. I'd look forward to testing myself on each topic to turn the topic green. This gamification of studying (and testing in particular) made it more motivating and enjoyable.

Other than testing myself more, another game-changing innovation was understanding spaced repetition. I used to think I was an idiot if I read something and then forgot it a few days later, but that's literally how our memory is supposed to work. Using spaced repetition, we can interrupt the Forgetting Curve (as you'll have learned about in this chapter), and so we're more likely to remember things.

Once I discovered the power of these evidence-based study techniques, I ended up doing better in my exams, while working and stressing a lot less. Because of all this copious free time, I ended up starting my YouTube channel while I was in medical school. That decision has completely changed my life (and is how I'm friends with Jade!), but it wouldn't have happened if I hadn't given these novel techniques a shot.

CHAPTER 4

STUDY
METHODS

This is the chapter I wish every school taught. How has the education system got away with expecting students to take exams to determine their future life prospects without ever actively teaching you *how* to study? We're given information. We're given textbooks. We're even taught each lesson in that textbook. But perhaps the most essential process – that of distilling, learning and memorising the content – is left up to you.

Let me tell you, it took me a long time to realise that highlighting my biology textbook wasn't going to get me an A* . . .

As I say, I'm no expert. But from all the research I've done on what makes revision effective, as well as what worked for me, I hope these techniques help optimise your time. Before reading this chapter, I highly recommend going back and reading chapter 3 so you are comfortable with the idea of SAAD study techniques. The SAAD framework gives you a base to understand why these revision techniques are so effective.

DITCH AESTHETICS

I know, I'm sorry. But you have permission to keep your pastel highlighters!

'Wow, those notes are beautiful, Jade!' my friend said, pointing to the class notes I'd just spent the day copying up. She pointed to the title, written once in pastel highlighter and lovingly written over again in fineline biro, the classic mark of an aesthetic Year 9 queen.

'Thank you,' I responded, smiling as I placed the sheet into my well-organised ringbinder.

By the time she asked, 'Can I see your flashcards?' I was already handing them to her.

Each flashcard was, as my oh-so-modest-self believed, beautiful. Tiny curled handwriting in full sentences. Every word had been laboured over, each flick of the pen in time to the pop music I was probably singing along to at the time.

My friend turned each one over in her hands to be met with more pretty squiggles and long lines. The block text was perfectly arranged.

The flashcard suddenly froze in her hand. She looked up at me. 'Isn't this exactly the same thing you wrote in class?'

I nodded. 'Sure, I mean, I changed the odd thing.' I took them back from her. 'But it's so much easier to revise from flashcards. It's way more effective for me when it looks pretty.'

She looked down at the thick block of text, no doubt thinking this was nothing better than a pretty version of the textbook.

What I didn't tell her was that though I felt great pride in my gorgeous notes, the thought of reading so much text filled me with dread. I didn't understand some of the topics and knew that these cards wouldn't change that. I could not recite a single card back to you from memory. After all, I had copied up sentences line-for-line.

That was me early in secondary school. Back then, though, tests were much simpler, so it didn't matter if my revision methods were effective or not.

Turns out, aesthetics are not scientifically backed to improve grades. Unfortunately.

I genuinely did not understand why flashcards were useful. I didn't know why directly copying my class notes onto a new piece of card was helpful. It turns out that I was missing the very point of flashcards. Instead of testing myself, summarising information and making my life easier, I was rereading diluted content which I may as well have read from a textbook – and saved myself a lot of time.

I have a deep respect for highlighters, especially pastel ones. But when it comes to how to revise, they aren't going to improve your grade. This chapter will show you ten scientifically backed SAAD revision methods which are less pretty but much more functional. If pretty notes truly make you happy, keep making them. But for the sake of your exams, do the following too.

As I went through school, I realised that doing well in an exam requires three main stages of studying. Whenever you come to revise, ask yourself which of the three stages below it fits into!

Understand → Learn → Apply

Without an initial grasp of the concepts, there is no point memorising the right words to string together in an exam question. The process of **understanding** begins in the classroom. It continues with reading study guides, watching videos, asking your teacher and peers for help, and wrestling with the content until you reach that 'ah-ha!' moment. It's not worth embarking on the memory-based revision techniques until you confidently understand the topic at hand. You need to be able to not only recall information but use it in new scenarios, so leverage the people and resources you have for that subject until you get it!

One of my biggest pieces of advice is to use class-time to just listen. During my A levels, I would skim over the lesson content in the textbook beforehand to familiarise myself with key terms. For the rest of that hour, I just listened, asked questions and tried to grasp the concept. It's tempting to only copy up notes during class but make your priority understanding, such as adding extra comments in your notebook to explain things in a way which makes sense for future you. It's much easier to teach yourself something at home when you know you've understood it before.

The second step is **learning**. It is one thing to finally understand something; it is another to be able to recall and retrieve specific information from the concept when prompted. When we read a textbook of concepts, we find ourselves nodding our head in agreement. The textbook makes sense. In fact, it seems easy. And yet suddenly, turning to an exam question on that very topic reveals the horrifying conclusion that you do not, in fact, *know* this information. Most people skip from the 'I understand' and go straight to the 'let's apply this in an exam' stage. Memorise, test yourself on, and learn, the content.

The third step is **application**. This is where you test yourself, pick up practice test papers and attempt to prove your knowledge in the way exams will reward you for. Practice papers elevate you from *knowing* the information to *using* it in the very specific way that exam boards want.

In this chapter, we are going to cover ten revision techniques which are tried and tested to help you thrive in the exams. Some of them require more time, others need a bit of creativity, but all of them work. They will take you through learning the information to applying it in the way you are going to need to do in your exams and assessments. It's important to actually try out these revision techniques to find out which ones work best for you. For each one that you master, you're adding to your study vocabulary. You're learning the language of revision so that by the time exam season hits, you're fluent.

All of these techniques hinge on creating SAAD revision, as discussed in chapter 3. Can you remember the elements of SAAD? Take a second to look away from the page and remind yourself. The process of actively recalling it is beneficial to long-term retention.

Here's a recap:

Spaced repetition is all about revisiting the same information at specific points in time to combat the forgetting curve of human memory. Recall information many times at the start and progressively less often as it enters your long-term memory.

Active recall means generating knowledge from your brain, even if it's hard. Instead of looking at the information on my flashcard, I write a question to force myself to produce the information myself.

Association means building on your prior knowledge. These techniques invite you to make connections between different topics to give you rich retrieval cues for the information.

Desirable difficulty means these techniques aren't going to be easy. Passive revision gives you a break. It's too easy and so you learn less. Instead, if you test yourself and wrestle with your knowledge in ways which reveal your difficulties you will ultimately learn the content in a much more meaningful way.

The harder your revision is, the easier the exams will be. Future You is already thanking you.

Before jumping into memorising content, here is a top, top, top tip to guide your revision! Make sure you're learning the right information. Print off the '**specification**' for your syllabus which can be found on the exam board's website. It has a long list of points from the people who write the exam papers and tells you what you *need* to know. For example, it might tell you that 'students should know how to round numbers to an appropriate degree of accuracy' in GCSE maths. The specification becomes a checklist of items to guide your revision. If you're working through the spec, you can walk into that exam hall confident that you've covered all the foundations. Use your textbook, class notes, teacher's notes and the specification to condense the most essential information that you'll need for that exam! *Spec*-tacular job, team.

Secondly, take a moment to '**diagnose**' your subjects and what they demand of you. This is one of the best things I do to guide my revision! Subjects like English literature are essay-based, so they require different revision methods to subjects like science which require you to apply your knowledge to short-answer questions. With some subjects, you can start anywhere. For example, geography allows you to study ideas, to some extent, in isolation – jumping across the map or from oxbow lake to volcanoes. However, some subjects build upon themselves such that you can't move onto the next concept before you have a solid understanding of the last. This is how maths works – if you're not confident in basic algebra, you'll struggle to do harder combined questions.

All of the revision techniques below are useful, but it's up to you to work out what your subjects require of you and use these techniques to help you. Do you need to memorise facts? Do you need to solve problems? Do you need to write essays? Get clear on how you will be marked and how your subject works!

As an example, let's **diagnose** GCSE English literature. What are the different parts that make up this subject, and what do they require you to do for revision? Here are some examples.

Requirement	Action
Be confident analysing and using different literary devices, e.g metaphors, alliteration	1. Memorise the names of enough literary devices and practise identifying them 2. Practise writing pieces and including literary devices
Know the conventions of different forms of text, e.g letter, poem, short story	1. Memorise conventions 2. Practise writing pieces using conventions 3. Practise analysing texts of each form
Know quotes from the set text and use them effectively to infer meaning	1. Memorise quotes 2. Practise analysing these quotes in an essay

You can similarly diagnose individual topics, chapters or exam papers within a subject to identify what you need to be able to do, and how you can tackle it. This chapter will give you techniques to help bridge the gap in an effective way. We'll come back to this diagnosis at the end and see how we should study.

Diagnosis done. Specification printed. Tentative smile on. Let's go learn!

LEARNING METHODS

1. Flashcards

One of the most common and most commonly *abused* revision techniques. If you think flashcards are a way to make a long-form 'revision version' of your class notes, I'm here to tell you that someone lied to you.

Flashcards should be three things: short, meaningful and connected.

Short, as in, short-short. As in, a few words on one flashcard. No long sentences, no overkill explanation, nothing that you can merely copy from your notes.

Flashcards are about making your life easy by condensing content into its bare bones. Think, how few words can you use to get your point across? The idea is that you already understand the concept, so you don't need to write a dissertation on a card. Instead, make it brief but meaningful. You should be able to fill in the blanks from the few words you've given yourself.

Flashcards are all about active engagement. If you're not filling in the blanks or explaining the concept to yourself using the prompts, you should be writing questions.

On one side of the flashcard, ask yourself a specific, directed question. For example:

Which is bigger and why? The phloem or the xylem.

This forces you to produce the basic answer but also to expand. Flip over the card, check whether or not you got it right, note down how you fared and then use specific spaced repetition methods to make sure you come back to this card again soon if you did poorly.

Flashcard language

Oh, this is fun. Without trying to, I developed my own flashcard language. Seeing words and parroting them back to yourself is great but you can make revision even more active by making yourself fill in the blanks. My flashcard language was made of various intuitive symbols. It made the process of writing cards more active, and was especially great when I was too lazy to write more. This is a way to force your brain to say aloud what the symbols mean. The more active recall, the better.

Increases = ↑

Decreases = ↓

Greater than or less than = < or >

Goes to = @

Therefore = ∴

Because = ∵

Shorten book character names by using symbols or letters, e.g. Othello = O

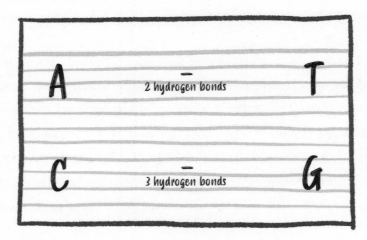

Shorten country or case study names with symbols or letters, e.g. India = In

For example, I would use the flashcard, on the previous page, to 'fill in' what each letter stands for in my head. This flashcard is a demonstration of DNA base pairings: I would fill in that A is adenosine and links with thymine (T) with two hydrogen bonds. If I wanted to make this even harder, I could leave a blank space where the number of hydrogen bonds is to force myself to recall this too.

For this flashcard, when I came to revise, I would cover up the text and just look at the prompt images to test myself on the reaction mechanisms. For example, I would look at the sun image and ask what it represents when thinking about ATP synthesis reactions. The sun makes me think of a process called photosynthesis which involves sunlight, which thus prompts my knowledge of phosphorylation. This process is especially helpful if you are a visual learner.

Covalent Bonds

Where are covalent bonds found?

How many covalent bonds can an atom make?

This flashcard has prompt questions to use active recall and features the answers on the back.

High Melting Point and Boiling Point

Lot of ENERGY needed to melt ...

∵
• Large number of strong electrostatic forces ... charge

• smaller the ion, the stronger the ionic bond; higher melting/ boiling point

• greater the charge, the stronger the ionic bonds; higher melting/ boiling point

This flashcard uses condensed symbols for the word 'because' and has blank spaces for me to fill in my knowledge. This turns the sentences into active recall prompts.

The beauty of flashcards is that they are straightforward to make and revise from. The downside is the discipline required to make them. I cannot recommend this enough: make flashcards as you go.

Get into the robust habit of making a flashcard for every meaningful topic you cover as you go. We all love pushing tasks to the end of the year but you will have enough on your plate when exams hit to be re-condensing old information. Do Future You a favour and learn to make useful flashcards from day one.

If you're reading this and exams are coming up, do not fret! There is still time. Dedicate time to the subjects you struggle with most first to get the biggest benefit out of flashcards.

You can make flashcards by hand or online using simple flashcard apps like Anki and Quizlet. These have the added benefit of inbuilt spaced repetition. After testing yourself on your knowledge, the app sorts the flashcard into different packs for revision. If you always get a concept right, you will not have to revisit that flashcard for a longer period. Equally, if you always forget the date that Henry VIII died, the app will make sure you're answering it every day until you know it.

However, you have to find what works best for you. If flashcard apps get you distracted, ditch them. If you always lose handwritten flashcards, consider using online cloud-based methods.

More than anything, start. Practice makes perfect with flashcards and their benefits are long-lasting. Remember, the more effort you put into simplifying information now, the easier life will be when you come to revise!

Here are some examples of how I designed flashcards:

Front of flashcard:

% Atom Economy

% Yield

NOTE: Always check equation is balanced

Back of flashcard:

$$\frac{\text{Mass of Desired Product}}{\text{Total Mass of Reactants}} \times 100$$

$$\frac{\text{Number of Moles/Mass of Specific Product}}{\text{Maximum Theoretical Moles/Mass of Product}} \times 100$$

- Yield can be lost by the practical process, or the practical not going to completion

Front of flashcard:

German

Langweilig

Wichtig

Lustig

Back of flashcard:

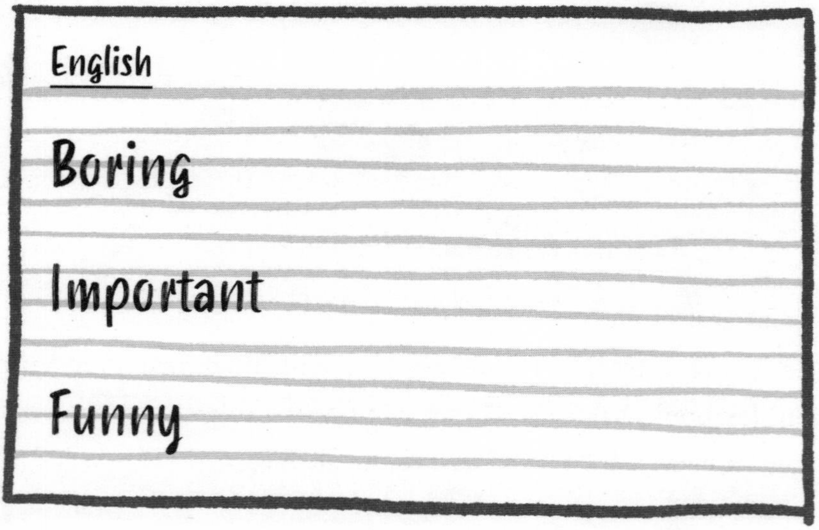

English

Boring

Important

Funny

For this flashcard, I would hide the text with my hand and test myself on each step using the images:

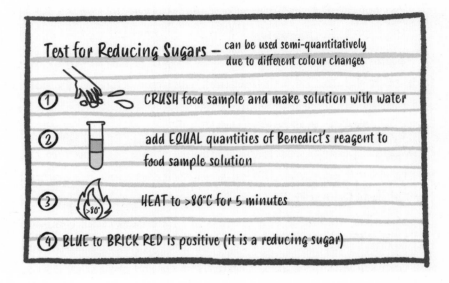

It's important to find a method that works for you but don't be fooled by the lure of aesthetics. As long as it's concise, meaningful and SAAD – it'll work in your favour.

Mini Challenge: Choose a line of the exam board specification for your subject and turn it into a flashcard. Be concise, meaningful and connect it to past knowledge. Reread this section to make sure it uses as much active recall as possible!

2. Summarisation from memory

We all love notes. It's the process of copying up information from your textbook, classes and revision guides in long-form sentences. Notes are easy to do, can be made while blaring loud music and require little mental effort.

And that's the issue.

Notes don't often fulfil the active recall element of SAAD revision and definitely don't equate to desirable difficulty. They're a useful foundation for further study but don't often count as revision themselves.

However, a friendly first step to studying if you *do* love note-taking is to summarise with intention. Take your lengthy class notes and aim to condense them into a few essential lines. The trick to make this effective is to do it half from memory. Read through your class notes, perhaps check the textbook, and when you feel like you've got a good grasp, challenge yourself to summarise without just copying. Even if you're summarising the information just a few minutes after reading it, this process of intentional recall is a good way to check your understanding, your ability to recall information and your knowledge of the key terms. If you can't remember how to spell 'Eyjafjallajökull volcano' or explain that five-slide PowerPoint in three summarised sentences, odds are you don't know it. Copying notes directly wouldn't have revealed that.

If physically writing the summary takes too long, you can say it aloud, either to yourself or explain it to a friend. Actively teaching someone is another useful way to test your understanding.

For example, watch a documentary related to a topic in your economics lesson, and then summarise the key facts from memory. Either write down your summary or tell a friend. This will test how well you understood the video as you are not copying up facts word-for-word. If you struggle to explain concepts to yourself, head to your textbook, read through the paragraphs and then summarise them again until you feel confident. This process might not teach you the exact wording the mark scheme needs, but it is very useful for the first stage of studying (understanding) and starting to learn the information.

Mini Challenge: Now that you just read through how to use two study techniques, summarise them to yourself or a friend in a few sentences. How do you make effective flashcards? What is summarisation? Why is it better than note-taking?

3. Chunking, chaining and telling a story

Chunking

In the cognitive neuroscience of memory, there is a useful technique for recall called 'Chunking'. Let's be honest, no one wants to memorise that 15-step process in physics. This method asks you to separate whatever information you're trying to learn into bitesized nuggets that you then create individual associations to. Each 'chunk' of information is made from dividing something large into small units which are related to each other, such as similar words, numbers or phrases. You actually do this naturally all the time because your brain can remember information better when it only needs to recall a few 'chunks'.

For example, the way that you remember your phone number is likely through Chunking. If your number is 01427548659, it is difficult to recall the seventh number from memory when asked. But if I asked you to give me your whole phone number, you have learned to repeat the whole thing in a practised way, such as 01427–548–659. You have naturally chunked it into three parts without trying. Repeat your phone number to yourself and notice if you have naturally chunked it into parts!

Equally in chapter 3 we learnt what makes a good evidence-based revision technique. With multiple aspects to human learning and lots of new information, it would be easy to leave this book and forget it all. Simply reading the text does not create footholds for you to remember long paragraphs. Instead, we broke all the information down into four elements, or four 'chunks', to create the simple acronym: S-A-A-D. Each letter prompts your knowledge of the information in that section, such as S being a chunk for spaced repetition. Now you only have to remember what each letter stands for to suddenly have access to the whole chapter.

This revision technique uses the second A of SAAD revision techniques – associations. You are creating a rich association to the knowledge through chunking it into something more accessible. This is why mnemonics and acronyms like SAAD are helpful ways to remember things.

Chaining

Imagine, you're trying to learn a historical event for a history exam. You know how it started and you know a few details about it, but you have no idea how they connect. The facts are scrambled in your head and, of all the subjects, in history it is pretty important to prioritise chronology. Welcome to Chaining. The idea is that you break down a process or event into a sequence of facts and associate each to the one before. Just as the question, 'How are you?' prompts a response like, 'Good', this technique is powerful because it means every fact naturally cues the recall of another.

Telling a Story

A way to use chaining and chunking together effectively is through storytelling. Creating a story forces you to break down lots of information into manageable pieces which connect to each other in a logical sequence. Give it a try:

1. Break down the process or event that you're trying to learn into five to ten key details.
2. Create a story linking the details in order.

Pretend you're telling a friend or sibling a summary of a novel or a bedtime fairy tale. If you're instead trying to learn a scientific process, treating essential facts like personified characters will add new depth to your learning.

Another reason that turning facts into a story is successful for long-term memory retention is because you are creating more associations. Here, each part of the story is logically chained to the last and cues your recall of the next.

Below is an example of storytelling to remember the process of water transport in the xylem. All keywords were taken from a mark scheme answer from a past paper in my syllabus. This is an effective way to remember an otherwise dull set of facts!

Example of storytelling: *The transport of water in the xylem*

*The clock struck **midday**, the **peak time** of water transportation in the plant. The **guard cells**, driven by an influx of water, conducted the grand opening of the **stomata** to a round of applause. Excited **water molecules** flew from the stomata in streams, thankful for the Queen of **Transpiration** letting them take on the journey from the soil to the surrounding air. As the* *first round of water molecules left, the plant sighed, grateful for the **lower pressure** at the top of the stem.*

*But this created **tension** in the xylem. Which water molecules would be chosen next to journey through the plant? They clung to each other in the xylem in anticipation. Each water molecule was special. Each was **dipolar**, hugging their neighbouring molecule with the companionable strength of **hydrogen bonding**. It was only because of the water molecules' **cohesion** that any of them would get to leave the stem; they had to work together.*

*'I hope it's **windy**,' one water molecule proclaimed.*

*'Oh yes, the **steeper the gradient**, the better the Queen of Transpiration's sister **Evaporation** will work.'*

*'I hope it's **sunny** today.'*

*'Me too! That would mean **more stomata** are **open**. The Queen of Transpiration will be even faster!'*

*As the water molecules travelled up the **dead cells** of the xylem tube like a straw, the long **root hair cells** at the bottom of the plant welcomed new water molecules through **osmosis**. And so, in a process as **passive** as the sun shining on the fields, the Queen of Transpiration pulled and water was taken up.*

The plant heaved a sigh of relief. It would live to be hydrated another day.

This technique truly makes revision fun. It is light-hearted, though admittedly time-consuming and not worth using for everything, but is a great way to break up long stints of working through past papers. You can also practise recalling the story through making mind-maps or flowcharts and connecting facts to one another from memory.

Storytelling counts as SAAD revision when the story is repeated often and in expanding intervals (spaced repetition), requires you to recall the characters and storyline from memory (active recall), is built on prior knowledge and chained to the next step of the story (association) and uses a storyline which appropriately distils what you need to learn (desirable difficulty). Happy storytelling!

Mini Challenge: Choose something that you've been struggling to learn and turn it into a story. Make awkward scientific terms the heroines, or business definitions the rules of an imaginary world!

4. Blurting

What sounds like your friend accidentally spilling secrets is actually the method that got me my A*s. Welcome to my **all-time favourite** technique. I was introduced to this by my wonderful A level biology teacher who made it a priority to mentor students in her free time about the importance of effective revision, without any prompting from my school. Shout out to you, Mrs Greenslade – you're the true revision queen.

Ever since I introduced this on my YouTube channel, I receive daily messages from students whose studying has been revolutionised by this active recall technique. Unlike passively highlighting text or rereading class notes, blurting is one of the most efficient and effective ways to understand where you are at in your knowledge – and do something about it.

To do this, take a concept or chapter you want to revise:

1. Write yourself a few **prompts** related to the topic to help jog your memory.
2. Without looking at any notes or your textbook, **write down everything you can remember** from that chapter. 'Blurt out'

all your knowledge from memory. Detail processes, list out vocabulary, define key terms. All of it. You can even set yourself a timer.

3. When you've written everything you can remember, **compare** your blurted knowledge to an official textbook, mark scheme or notes. Suddenly, you've got evidential proof of what you do and don't know.

Did you recall things word for word? Were you *actually* able to explain that difficult concept or did you just think you knew it? What did you leave out?

Blurting is easy to put off because it is mentally taxing. It forces you to stare your knowledge in the face and be honest with where you're at, without the luxury of hiding behind a textbook. However, it is an essential self-assessment tool to show you what you need to spend more time on. The more you repeat blurting the same concepts, the stronger your knowledge in them will become.

Blurting became my go-to technique for almost any subject. From recalling maths formulas to drama practitioners' theories, it saved me time and forced me to consolidate my knowledge.

Example:

To revise the process of river meander formation in geography, I've identified the following prompts of the chapter:

- *Oxbow lakes*
- *Erosion*
- *Sediment*

Blurted knowledge:

- *The river's force causes the sides of the river to change shape. The higher the force, the more it changes shape. On the side with less force, there is more sediment.*
- *Over time, a meander forms.*
- *If the meander continues forming, it might become an oxbow lake.*

Comparison to official notes:

- *The force of the water **erodes** and undercuts the river bank on the **outside** of the bend where water flow has most energy **due to decreased friction**.*
- *On the **inside** of the bend, where the **river flow is slower**, material is **deposited** as sediment, as there is **more friction**.*
- *Over time, the horseshoe becomes tighter, until the ends come very close together. As the river breaks through, **e.g. during a flood**, the loop is cut off from the main channel. The cut-off loop is called an oxbow lake.*

Here, I can see that my knowledge of meander formation was shallow. So I need to go back and revise how 'friction' is a causal factor; the differences between the 'inside' and 'outside' river bank and to include key terms like 'deposited'. Without blurting my knowledge using active recall, I would not have known that I lacked this specificity. Now that I'm aware of the gaps in my knowledge, I can revise more effectively and try this process again tomorrow.

Mini Challenge: Choose a chapter from any subject and practise Blurting by writing down everything you can remember! Check your notes to see if you forgot any keywords.

5. Sherlock's Mind Palace

Yes, you read that right. Sherlock, as in, Sherlock Holmes. Who better to learn from than the fictional mastermind and genius detective?

This technique is one of the most creative and effective I've ever tried, if used correctly. It's best for memorising long processes, definitions that must be remembered word-for-word (did someone say science mark schemes?) and anchoring difficult-to-remember ideas to something more concrete.

The idea is that you associate a word or sentence to a specific object or action. You anchor each part of a concept repeatedly until it is ingrained in your memory. When you need to recall the information, you use the objects or actions as a prompt to list off each element of the concept.

Sherlock used this to remember small details by chaining information to a space he knew by heart: his house. He would imagine himself walking through his home, with each object in the room prompting a different fact. If he needed to remember a difficult piece of information, he could simply close his eyes and imagine his house, walking himself through the rooms of prompts. Suddenly, each detail would come back to him.

This is also why a person's face triggers recall of their name. Your brain has actively associated their appearance to that word. And it is how you're able to remember the words for different objects in another language: you learn to connect the word 'chair' to any physical object in that shape.

Shakespeare's actors used this technique to remember their lines in The Globe theatre. Actors engaged in a slow process of associating each line with a different detail of the theatre. Tracing their eyes down the left side of the furthest column might remind them of the words 'To be or not to be', while drawing their eyes along the next edge of the column reminded them of the other character's next line. This is how actors were able to memorise a new play in only a day.

Now, I'm not saying you have to learn an entire Shakespeare play in one day to be (or not to be) a genius, but it is worth testing out this technique the next time you want to learn something lengthy!

This technique is built on the two As of SAAD revision – active recall and association. Through associating new concepts to your existing knowledge of a physical space, you are creating rich retrieval cues to recall the information.

Processes

Let's try and remember the following A level politics process using Sherlock's Mind Palace. This process details how a new law is made in the UK Parliament.

The process of a Bill becoming an Act of Parliament:

1. **Draft Bill**: a draft is issued for consultation before being formally introduced to Parliament. This allows changes and amendments to be made.
2. **First reading**: the Bill is introduced (read out) to Parliament, with no debate or voting.
3. **Second reading**: a full debate takes place considering the details of the Bill.
4. **Committee stage**: a public committee of MPs can make amendments to the Bill.
5. **Report stage**: the committee reports its amendments to the Commons, which can agree to, or reverse, any changes.

6. **Third reading**: this is another full debate of the Bill but no amendments can be made, usually Bills will be passed at this stage.
7. **Second chamber**: once the Bill is passed by the Commons, the same process takes place in the House of Lords.
8. **Royal assent**: once passed by both chambers, the Bill is given to the monarch to grant royal assent. Once this happens, the Bill becomes law.

Wow. Hefty, right? The thought of learning a long process like this can feel overwhelming. Let's break it down.

So you need to remember the eight stages: draft Bill, first reading, second reading, committee stage, report stage, third reading, second chamber and royal assent. In that order.

To do this, imagine a space you know by heart. This could be your bedroom, your house, your garden or a school classroom. Let's imagine using your house.

Imagine approaching your front door. Before you can put the key in the lock, you have to repeat to yourself, 'draft Bill'. You can imagine yourself pretending to open your door like a draft of the real thing. The image of your front door is the first cue.

Imagine yourself turning the key once: **first reading**. Nothing happens with only one turn of the key, just like no debates happen within the first reading of a new Bill in Parliament. Then turn the key again: **second reading**. The door opens and you can go through, just like Parliament will debate the Bill on the second reading so it can go through to the next stage.

Enter your hallway, or whatever room comes first in your house. Imagine your family members gathering to greet you as you come in: **committee stage**. A group of people discuss and make changes to the Bill, just like you and your family might discuss the day you've just had.

When you see your family, you report how you feel to them: **report stage**. Your family can make changes to your mood, just like the Commons can make changes to the Bill once amendments are reported.

Imagine yourself leaving the hallway and approaching the next door. You reach for the handle and turn it: **third reading**. You no longer talk to your family and no changes can be made to what you said, just like how no further changes can be made to the Bill at this stage.

You enter the next room: **second chamber**. This space is different than your hallway, just like the House of Lords is different to the House of Commons.

Finally, imagine going to sit on your sofa and feeling like a king or queen as you relax after a long day: **royal assent**. Once passing both chambers, or both rooms in your house, the monarch confirms the Bill and it becomes law.

Suddenly, you have connected a process in its correct order to somewhere you know well. There is no way you can get the order mixed up because you are familiar with the order of rooms in your house. The process of how a Bill becomes law is much more likely to stick in your long-term memory due to the rich retrieval cues you've created. Every time you come home after school, you can even repeat it to yourself because using spaced repetition will lodge it firmly in your long-term memory. In an exam, you can now close your eyes and simply imagine the journey through your house to recall the entire process.

Facts

As you can see, Sherlock's Mind Palace is incredible for learning processes. However, one of the reasons Sherlock was able to remember so many niche facts was through associating them to different objects in his house. When you have abstract statistics, it is important to ground them in something physical if you're going to remember them. For example, I could choose the mirror by my bed as the first object. From now on, this mirror is associated with the fact, 'The UK economy's GDP growth in 2016 was 1.8 per cent'. Sounds dry. Sounds complex. But if every time you look at your mirror for the next few months you repeat this fact to yourself, it will become second nature. You can even put a Post-it note on your mirror with this fact on it so you can check your knowledge every day. The idea is that Sherlock could mentally walk through his house in his mind and recall a fact with every object he pointed at. If you are a visual or spatial learner, this is incredibly effective!

Though it might seem like an unnecessarily long process to create the retrieval cues, you are saving time in the long run. Highlighting the same process in a textbook 50 times won't give you the foundation to recall it. Take the time now and you'll be so grateful when you see an exam question on exactly that process!

6. Object association: An extension of the Mind Palace

It's not just things in your home that can be used to help you remember facts and processes – think about the individual details of any object you know well, even those you'll have in the exam hall. Object association is powerful when you successfully link any abstract idea you need to remember to something physical you know well. In other words, that rubber in your pencil case could be the secret to an A*!

When I learned about this technique, I started using objects I knew I would have with me during the exam. For example, I could remember key details about D&T iterative design from the different parts of my water bottle and the process of electromagnetic conduction from the lines of my pencil. Let me take you through how I learned the exact, word-for-word definition of the enthalpy of combustion using my pointer finger.

Funny story. When I began writing this book, I hadn't recalled this definition in two and a half years. Just for fun, I thought I'd test out my recall before reviewing the definition.

I grabbed a piece of paper and took my brain through the process I built on object association using my finger for my A level chemistry exam, writing out every word I could remember.

Here it is:

> The standard enthalpy change when one mole of a compound is burned completely in oxygen under standard conditions, all reactants and products being in their standard states.

When I was finished, I checked my dusty revision notes and confirmed that I am the biggest nerd of all time. I know it almost word-for-word to this day. That is the long-term power of object association. Get ready to get creative.

I wanted to remember the following definition:

'The standard **enthalpy change of combustion** is the **enthalpy change** when **one mole of a compound** is **burned completely** in **oxygen** under **standard conditions**, **all** reactants and products being in their **standard states**.'

Every element of this definition is necessary to receive full marks from the AQA exam board in A level chemistry, so I needed to put each word accurately into my long-term memory.

Now what object did I know I'd have in the exam hall?

My hand.

I can feel you laughing at my insanity. Don't worry, I am too! Just remember that this technique was so useful I can still remember this rather dry definition to this day.

Here we have my finger.

The first phrase in the definition that I wanted to remember was: 'The standard enthalpy of combustion is the enthalpy change . . .'

For this, I traced around the tip of my finger in a circle. The concept of 'enthalpy change' refers to energy and thermodynamics and the movement of circling reminded me of an energetic change, making it memorable. I imagined that touching my finger to fire (related to combustion) would start this process.

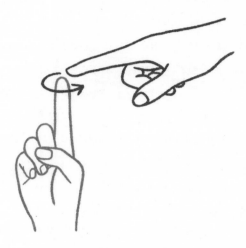

The next line is 'when one mole of a compound'. When I ran my finger down my pointed finger, I would remember '**one mole of compound being combusted**'.

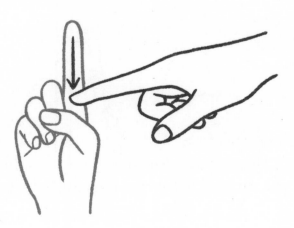

The next part 'is burned completely in oxygen' was associated with me tracing the shape of a circle around the base of my finger in the shape of an 'O' for the element oxygen.

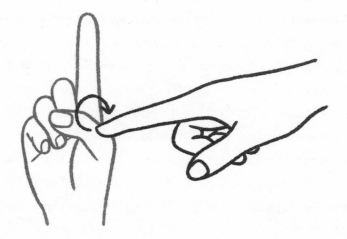

To remember the essential phrase 'under standard conditions', I turned my hand around, still keeping my finger pointed, and traced my knuckle on the other side.

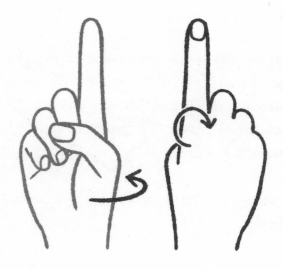

To end the movement, I repeated what I did at the beginning in reverse by tracing a line up my finger to represent 'all reactants and products being in their standard states' and ended on tracing a circle above my fingertip. Going back to the start was a symbolic way for me to remember that everything involved in the process was also in its initial 'beginning' state.

Now, imagine I open the exam paper and see a gorgeous three-mark question asking for the definition of the 'enthalpy change of combustion'. I can simply trace round my finger and recall each line of the definition, word for word, with ease.

I'd circle the fingertip, trace down the finger in a one shape, draw the O shape for oxygen, turn my hand and get it back to its 'original state'. With each brush of my fingers, the words of the definition returned. I used to practise this process every day until I could do it in my sleep.

Let's take another definition to practise. Seeing as this is the most dramatic technique of all time, it seems fitting to take an example from A level drama. Imagine we want to remember the definition of the alienation effect:

Alienation effect: **Theatrical techniques** designed to **remind the audience** that they are watching a play and so **distance** them from **identifying emotionally** with the **characters and events** depicted. Central to the dramatic theories of **Bertolt Brecht**.

Here is an object that you will likely have in your exam: a simple pencil.

From now on, start associating your pencil with the image of an alien to cue recall of the alienation effect. You can imagine pencil-shaped aliens or using the pencil to draw an alien.

To recall the first words, 'theatrical techniques', you can move your finger around the tip of the pencil dramatically. Every time you circle it with pizazz, think of being on stage in a theatre. Then lightly prod the sharp pencil tip into the pad of your finger as though 'reminding the audience' that the theatre isn't real. Move your finger down the entire length of the pencil to 'distance' the audience from the dramatic emotions at the tip. For the final part of the definition, you can associate the rubber at one end with removing any 'emotional' attachment the audience has to the play, as though rubbing it away. Finally, to me, the name 'Brecht' reminds me of 'break', so I would imagine the pencil lead breaking to remind me of this theatre practitioner. 'Breaking' the pencil is also a reminder of breaking the audience's attachment to the play.

Now, when asked to recall this definition, I can dramatically circle the tip of the pencil, lightly press the point on my finger, distance my finger to the other end of the pencil and then touch the rubber to remind me of the last phrase, before imagining the pencil breaking. With ease, I just associated a lengthy definition to a retrieval cue I will have in the exam.

Why does this strange technique work? Coming back to the framework of SAAD revision techniques, this is grounded in association as it requires you to create rich retrieval cues and bring them back into your mind using active recall. Especially at the start, it is desirably difficult to remember the entire definition, so your brain must work actively.

Try it yourself on that definition you always forget or the process you feel like you have no hope of remembering. Focus on the keywords and start adding the parts of the definition piece by piece to areas on an object in front of you. How can you connect the words and phrases you need to know to the parts of the object? I recommend taking ten minutes to associate the concept with an object or even your hand to creatively insert it into your long-term memory. Practise recalling one more step each time. Eventually, you'll stop checking the definition and instead just use the object to remember the phrases. Use spaced repetition to reinforce your associated concept regularly until you don't even have to think about it anymore.

You only have so many objects and well-known places to use, so use this sparingly but know that is highly effective.

You've got this, Sherlock.

APPLICATION

Now that you've had a go at more deeply *learning* the information, it's time for the part that will get you marks: application. You see, most exam papers don't just ask you to recall a few definitions and repeat them for top grades. The best marks come from answering questions which don't always have obvious answers. It might be a brand new essay question asking about a book character who only appears in one chapter. It might be a maths question which looks *impossible*, only because it's hiding that it wants you to use a process you know very well. To bridge the gap between just knowing the information, and being able to retrieve it and *use* it, we need to practise application. This is Desirably Difficult after learning the content – an important part of SAAD revision techniques. This section will go through the different ways of testing your existing knowledge, such as using textbook questions, past papers and writing essays.

Remember, the academic system is a game. The players: you and the exam boards.

The nature of the game is that even if you know the concepts, you only score a point if it's written the exact way the exam board has specified. It doesn't matter if you have a niche understanding of the physics of supernova stars or artistic skills worthy of display in the Louvre, if you don't present your knowledge how the mark scheme wants you to, you won't win. Now, I could write a whole book about how this is problematic; about how we're not encouraged to think critically but confine ourselves to parroting information in a set way – which is no way to measure intelligence or foster curiosity.

However, like I said, this is a game. You are a player. And you came to win.

Winning is about understanding exactly what the exam board wants and giving it to them. The only way you can do this is to familiarise yourself with the language they use, the words they want to hear and how questions are structured. The solution? Past papers.

Past paper questions differ between essay, practical and mathematical subjects. There are both short-form and long-form questions to tackle. You can find past papers on the exam boards' website, in your end of chapter tests at school and on legacy sites which compile resources (ask your teacher if they know any for your subject!). We'll also go through different ways of accessing questions and, most importantly, how to get the most out of the process.

If you just do one thing after reading this book, pick up past papers. Make mark schemes your lifeblood and examiners' reports your bedtime reading – just kidding, bit overkill. But using past paper questions? That's how you'll smash those exams.

7. Textbook questions and revision guides

But before you leap right into past papers, start by using the first application resource at your disposal. Every textbook for your syllabus should provide practice questions as you're learning the content. These are a great way to test your knowledge on the ground. After every class, make sure you can answer these questions, either on paper or in your head. The answers can often be found at the back of the textbook and are useful to check in with yourself. Did you *actually* understand the lesson? If you're struggling either reread your notes or ask a teacher for help.

Also make use of revision guides for your exam board. Choose up-to-date ones that map to your curriculum, are relatively short and easy-to-use, but beware the cringey puns you find in so many of them! Plus, remember they're a starting point but not necessarily the way of accessing the highest grades. Make it a habit to revisit textbook and revision guide questions even months after you covered the material in class. Due to the forgetting curve of human memory discussed back in chapter 3, you'd be surprised how differently you approach them with time. Regularly revisit these bite-sized questions to refresh your understanding. The most important tip is not to read your notes or a lesson summary before answering the questions (even though it's tempting!). In doing so, you'll only be testing your short-term memory and you want to know what is already lodged in your brain.

If you are doing these questions before you have done much revision it will probably mean you don't know that many of the answers. That's totally fine. The process of sitting down and dragging information back to your mind is strengthening the synaptic connections in your brain to that old knowledge. You're telling your brain to sort through its many ring-binder folders of concepts in search of the right one. You can read the lesson summary afterwards to see what your brain didn't manage to retrieve for you.

Top tips for practice questions

When practising questions in the textbook, get good at recognising the command words. These are the first verbs you see, and they normally require different things. It's like a hint from the exam board about what they are asking of you. Here are some common ones below and what they mean:

- **State**, e.g. *State the definition on the enthalpy change of combustion.*

  The exam boards want you to 'express in clear terms'. This answer normally does not require *why, how* or an *example.* Simply write down the definition you've learned with as many key words as possible. If it's 2 marks, make sure to write down at least 2 statements. If it's 3 marks, write down 3 and so on. Other command words with a similar meaning: *Give, identify, outline*

- **Explain**, e.g. *Using Figure 12 and your own knowledge, explain how different landforms may be created by the transport and deposition of sediment along the coast.*

  Explain questions are beasts! Here, they don't just want you to list out your knowledge – they want you to detail 'purposes or reasons', work out why something is the way it is and discuss the causal factors. Again, if it's a 3-mark question, write at least 3 points!

- **Describe**, e.g. *Describe examples of women's work during the First World War.*

  Unlike explaining *why* or *how* something is the way it is, describing merely means stating what is there and laying out characteristics.

- **Justify**, e.g. *'Transnational corporations (TNCs) only bring advantages to the host country.' Do you agree with this statement? Justify your decision.*

  This type of question could be worth many marks and often involves ethical debates. When you see this word, make sure to support a case with evidence.

- **To what extent**, e.g. *To what extent do urban areas in lower income countries (LICs) or newly emerging economies (NEEs) provide social and economic opportunities for people?*

  For subjects like geography, this command phrase is asking you to judge the importance or success of a strategy, scheme or project. For subjects like English literature, it's asking you to weigh up how much you agree with something.

Add in some spaced repetition to elevate your long-term retention. Repeat these questions again at increasingly longer intervals. Sad questions just became a SAAD revision technique!

8. Practice essays

Throwback to A level English literature. There's nothing I wanted to do less than go through the effort of writing a whole essay. It was taxing enough to memorise book quotes or page references, analyse and re-analyse poems and read a novel for the hundredth time. Did somebody say *Wuthering Heights? The Great Gatsby? Of Mice and Men?* I love literature but there's something about studying books in school that butchers the fun of reading.

However, the best thing to do to get you ready for exams in essay subjects is, you've guessed it, write essays.

There are so many elements to writing a good essay, from the organisational structure, to getting the timing right, to creating an optimal essay outline, to including enough quotations or references. Let alone worrying if the content is creative or relevant to the question.

How to write practice essays for any subject

- **Use past paper questions**. I recommend saving the most recent papers to practise with near to your real exam but any other questions you can get hold of are worth using. For English literature, you want to be well prepared for questions related to characters, themes, settings and relevant historical events. If you can't find a past paper question that tackles all of these elements, either create one yourself or ask your teacher to prepare you a practice question.

- **Always time yourself**. Even in the early days or if you're just practising essay-writing for quality rather than an exam scenario, it is useful to measure how long it roughly takes you to process the question.

- **Always plan your essay**. Write an outline, pick apart quotes of choice, create a running thread to tie the essay together and give yourself a helpful roadmap. I know many people who don't plan essays. There was a time when I was one of them. But I can wholeheartedly say that planned essays are better essays. Even if you meander, spontaneously add points or go in a new direction, the clarity of an overall plan is essential, especially under timed conditions.
- **Organisation and structure**. Following on from creating a plan, your essay should have a clear, easy-to-follow structure. Think about travelling to Paris. You want to follow regular, logical sign-posts to get you from A to B. You know what your destination is the whole time, and all the travel routes on the way are supporting the journey. An essay without a structure is like aiming for Paris but taking a hundred detours and ending up at the fake Eiffel Tower in Las Vegas. Just not as magical.

How you structure your essay depends on the conventions of the subject, the topic and number of marks in a given question. Every essay has a macro structure and a micro structure. The macro structure is its overall formation. It is how your essay flows at a high level. We love a solid **introduction** or topic sentence, **body paragraphs** which explore your idea using lots of evidence, and a gorgeous **conclusion** which ties together all your points in a summary, without adding anything new.

Ask your teacher for specific advice about the best structure for your subject. For example, a comparative essay between two texts could use a diamond macro structure like this:

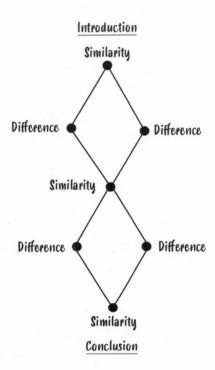

Introduction
Similarity
Difference   Difference
Similarity
Difference   Difference
Similarity
Conclusion

In this structure, each black dot represents a well-written body paragraph. What makes it a successful comparison is that we are consistently digging into the similarities with evidence from both texts, discussing differences between them with an in-depth analysis of each, and once again tying it all together with the given question.

The **micro** structure of an essay is how each of these body paragraphs are written. There are many frameworks you can use to be successful, but it's always a good idea to introduce a relevant point with a topic sentence, back it up with evidence, and then provide an in-depth explanation of why it answers the question. This basic structure is often referred to as **PEEL** – Point, Evidence, Explanation and Link back to the question.

P – Point: Introduce the topic you are going to discuss in this paragraph with one clear sentence.

E – Evidence: Support your point with examples, such as facts and statistics, figures, research findings, and quotes from the text. Choose evidence you can expand upon.

E – Explanation: Show your understanding of how your given evidence supports the main point and why you have a strong argument.

L – Link to the question or context: Reinforce your original point and make sure it is relevant to the given question. You can also provide a transition to the next topic or paragraph.

The most essential part of any PEEL paragraph is the explanation, where you dig into why your chosen evidence supports your argument. Let's look at an example.

The question is: Should animals be kept in zoos?

P: It is **cruel to take animals away from their natural habitats.**

E: **As shown in the text**, studies suggest that **animals kept in captivity become bored**. They can also develop a condition called '**zoochosis**' where they anxiously rock back and forth.

E: The fact that animals develop these conditions in captivity, but not in the wild, **suggests they are not meant to be kept in restrictive enclosures.** Even if zoos are enjoyable for humans, they cause suffering to the animals in them.

L: Therefore, animals **should not be kept in zoos because** it is cruel to subject to them to inevitable suffering.

This very simple paragraph has been broken down into its PEEL structure. The explanation could be further developed, such as considering the alternative side of human enjoyment in more depth, but overall this framework ensured that the given question was approached with credible evidence.

To access higher marks, the PEEL structure is just your starting point. It is important to be flexible and use more than one piece of evidence for the same point. For example, one way to creatively reach higher marks in English is to begin by identifying the literary device as your 'evidence', but then develop your argument with word-level analysis, sentence structure analysis or alternative interpretations. This will hammer home the point you are making!

Ask your teacher for advice on which macro and micro structure works best for the demands of your subject. Whatever you do, make sure you are factoring organisational structure into how you write your essays. Point me in the direction of the *real* Eiffel Tower.

- **Always use a range of words for 'suggests'.** When your essay hinges on use of sources, figures or literary texts, the odds are you will have to infer meaning from them. Rather than repeating the same word (Pikachu, I choose you! Again . . .), memorise a list of sophisticated synonyms. Such as highlights, shows that, signifies, connotes, indicates, implies, proves that.
- **Always ask someone to give you feedback on your essay**. Half the learning is writing the essay. The other half is understanding how you actually did. There's a beautiful bias called 'The Ikea Effect', inspired by the store's flatpack furniture that customers have to build themselves using a set of instructions. Research has shown that humans always overvalue their own creations and an Ikea customer will value the table they put together themselves over an identical table they purchased

ready-made (because clearly that wonky cabinet your dad put together is art). Similarly, you will overvalue an essay you've written more than one written by someone else. So to overcome this, you need an objective second opinion. I understand it can feel scary, or seem like extra work, to reach out to a teacher and ask them to review your essay, but you need to do it. There is nothing more valuable than tangible feedback on your writing. Unlike science or maths, where answers are defined by a mark scheme, essay-based subjects are wonderfully subjective.

Top tip for essays: Relevance

When you have so many good ideas and things to talk about, it's easy to write an essay that answers the question you *wanted* to be asked as opposed to the one that is actually on the paper (because yes, if I write an essay about different breeds of dog, I will get full marks!). Relevance is one of the most important elements of a good essay response. I learned this the hard way! No matter how many quotes, historical evidence or fancy vocabulary you include, if it doesn't answer the given question, it won't get you the marks. I recommend **starting and ending every paragraph** with a **direct tie-in to the question**. Find ways of rewording the essay question into your response and make sure it remains central to the points you are making.

For example, if the question asks, 'Explain how Shakespeare created **feelings of guilt** in Act 1, Scene 2 of *Othello*' you can start your paragraph with, '**Shakespeare's use of** XYZ helps the audience **feel** a sense of **guilt** in this scene.' The next paragraph could start with, 'The stage directions in **Act 1, Scene 2** use body language to demonstrate Desdemona's **feelings of guilt** to the audience . . .'

This will keep you on track, as it will remind you what you are supposed to be writing about, and it will highlight to the examiner that you are directly addressing the question you've been asked.

9. Timed essay plan

So maybe you don't have time to write a whole essay. That's okay. You're not lazy, you might just be smart. One of my favourite revision techniques is planning an essay exactly as though you're going to write it, including all the relevant quotations and trains of thought. And time it. Force yourself to pretend that you will answer this question in an exam scenario.

Not only does this teach you to streamline your essay outlines to a set time (e.g. five minutes), but you are using active recall of your existing knowledge to approach the given question, whether you write the full essay or not.

But that's the thing, how do you write a good essay plan?

I remember asking my GCSE English teacher that exact question in Year 10. Up until then, I'd been winging essays. They were a fun combination of spontaneous thoughts and shoving in anything relevant like I was playing whack-a-mole.

The most useful first step to learning to plan essays is to start at the end. Take an existing essay you've written, preferably one which got a good mark, and deconstruct it to see how you structured it. In other words, produce an essay plan based on the essay you have already written, rather than the other way around. This 'reverse outline' is useful to identify how your thoughts evolved, which pieces of evidence you brought in to support your points and ultimately if your essay is coherent. This is an efficient way to assess how well you built on your ideas – or, conversely, scattered them.

Now look at your reverse outline and think about what it shows you about what you put into your essay. You normally have an introduction, or at least a topic sentence, body paragraphs that present and build upon related ideas and a conclusion that relates everything back to the question and ties up your analysis with a bow. Are these elements present and are they working well together? Have you used enough evidence? Notice whether the paragraphs link well to one other or if there are big jumps or loose ends.

This book is not aiming to teach you how to write a good essay; this is a nuanced art that varies from subject to subject and person to person. You would really need a whole book to cover that (they do exist!) but in the time it takes you to read it you could be practising you own essay questions and developing your technique. And it was definitely consistently practising essay plans and deconstructing my essays after I'd written them that helped me get the top percentage in essay-based subjects.

Challenge yourself. Put away the notes and the distractions, set a timer and plan a new essay. You'll learn a lot.

10· Past papers – and how to learn from them

To write this, I just watched the video I made on past papers when I was 17. BABY ME WAS SO CUTE. I've lost count of the number of times I nervously flicked my hair. It's funny how we grow and evolve.

Regardless of Mini Jade's hair-flicking, she had some decent points.

Past papers are the most under-used resource in the game, and not because we don't do them but because we're not taught how to *learn* from doing them. Ultimately, it doesn't matter if you get 80 per cent or 30 per cent. This actually says little about how good you are. It's all about what you do next.

How will you use this incredible evaluation tool to learn what you didn't know?

Make it a habit to do more with your end of chapter tests than simply reading them and shoving them in a drawer. Most end of chapter tests are made up of old past paper questions, so learning from them is like gold dust. They are a hint of what your real exam will look like, from the wording of the mark scheme, to the layout, to the types of questions. Schedule a meeting with your teacher to go through any questions you got wrong, particularly when you still don't understand how to get full marks. You can even ask to do end of chapter papers *again* a few weeks later just to make sure you understand everything.

One framework I used to evaluate my past papers, especially in science subjects, was the acronym MARCKS. Shoutout to my biology teacher again for this one.

Each letter is an explanation for why you lost the mark. How can you fix your knowledge unless you know why it went wrong?

After every test, I'd make it a habit to spend three minutes flicking through my past paper, marking every question with a letter as to why I got it wrong. The MARCKS acronym became so deeply ingrained in my head that I would scribble 'M's and 'C's and 'R's on my paper with ease.

M – Maths error

You got a question wrong due to an issue with your maths. Maybe it was a silly mistake with the numbers or you didn't know the formula.

A – Application

You lost the mark because you didn't understand the application context of the question. These questions are generally worth the most marks and understandably challenging.

R – Read the question (RTQ)

Otherwise known as a silly mistake. R means you didn't read the specifics of the question. Did you answer another essay question? Or define a different process?

C – Communication

You knew your stuff. You were on the right lines. But you did not express your thoughts sufficiently clearly.

K – Knowledge

You just don't know the content in this topic well enough. I recommend going back to number five in the learning methods earlier and blurting your knowledge to identify gaps in it.

S – Statement

The question was a 2-marker but you only gave one point. Or the question was a whopping 6-marker and you only wrote two lines. This reason is easy to fix but equally annoying when done wrong. Always check the number of marks on offer!

After hastily marking your past paper under this framework, tally up how many of each letter you wrote. All of a sudden, you now know the primary reason this paper went wrong. Whether your maths knowledge is the reason you lost marks, or you never wrote enough statements to get all the points, you can work on this for the next past paper you do.

The final and most important step is to write yourself a summary note on the front of the paper with action items. Based on your MARCKS analysis, what will you do now?

For example, 'practice questions on chapter 6' or 'go over this definition'.

Moving these action items from your paper to your to-do list is the only way they'll get tackled. For every past paper you do, don't miss out on the opportunity to learn from it. It'll help you out, I promise.

If you don't study science, you can easily come up with a similar framework to evaluate your past papers with. Identify common reasons you lose marks, perhaps relating to specific topics or concepts, and tally them up. *This* is where you need to focus your energy.

Mini challenge: go through a past paper or end of chapter test that you did recently and evaluate it using the MARCKS framework. What is the main reason you lost marks? How can you change your revision strategy to go through these areas in more depth?

PAST PAPERS ARE THE NEW TEXTBOOK

Finally, I recommend using past paper mark schemes and examiners' reports to inform your flashcards and notes. They can be found for free online if you search the exam board and subject. If you're going to invest so much time and energy memorising information, it better be the right information.

Work the mark scheme into your summarised notes. For example, when I made flashcards about a certain topic, I would skim through past papers to find questions related to that topic. You can use Control-F on your laptop as a shortcut key to search key terms from that chapter and see if there are questions about it.

Remember, if exams are a game, it's not just about how *much* you know but how you express what you know in the way they want. Become one with the mark scheme.

And there you have it! My top ten SAAD-approved revision recommendations to make the most out of your study time. We love highlighting, sure. We love rereading, yes. But your grades won't love it. Unfortunately, your knowledge won't just appear unless you work for it. So test out these techniques and find out which ones work best for you. You've got this.

If you have revision techniques which work for you but aren't listed here – that's great! Ask yourself, **does it fit into the Understanding, Learning or Application phase of studying?** Use the **SAAD** Framework from chapter 3 to make sure it's effectively optimising how you learn.

I dare you to go and practise one of the new revision techniques above. Test it out on something you've been struggling to remember for a while, or apply your knowledge in a past paper if you're feeling confident.

Before we move on, let's come back to our initial diagnosis of English literature at the start of this chapter and work out how we would use these techniques to tackle it!

Through identifying the phase of revision of each requirement (Understand, Learn or Apply) and specific techniques to tackle it, you are one step closer to planning effective revision!

Requirement	Action	Phase of Revision? (Understand/ Learn/Apply)	Revision Techniques
Be confident analysing and using different literary devices, e.g metaphors, alliteration	1. Memorise the names of enough literary devices and practise identifying them 2. Practise writing pieces and including literary devices	1. **Understand** and **Learn** 2. **Apply**	1. **Flashcards**. On one side, write an example of the literary device being used, and then flip it over to see the name. This uses active recall and spaced repetition when repeated at set intervals! 2. **Practise Essays** and **Essay Plans.** This moves onto the application phase and is of desirable difficulty. Write essays analysing the use of literary techniques, or creative writing pieces to practise using them! Get a teacher to give you feedback
Know the conventions of different forms of text, e.g letter, poem, short story	1. Memorise conventions 2. Practise writing pieces using conventions 3. Practise analysing texts of each form	1. **Learn** 2. **Apply** 3. **Apply**	1. **Flashcards** or **Blurting** 2. **Practise essays** 3. **Practise essays**
Know quotes from the set text and use them effectively to infer meaning	1. Memorise quotes 2. Practise analysing these quotes in an essay	1. **Learn** 2. **Apply**	1. **Flashcards, Blurting, Chaining and Storytelling, Object Association** to learn quotes. Repeat quotes to yourself regularly using spaced repetition 2. Practise essay and essay plans

PUT IT IN PRACTICE:

- Diagnose a subject or chapter of choice. What do you need to be able to do? Understand processes? Recall facts? Analyse and use certain techniques?
- Ask yourself which phase of revision each requirement is in.
- Identify which revision techniques are best suited to this action.
- Most of all, try out the techniques! Get confident in everything from blurting, to making effective flashcards, to analysing past papers with the MARCKS framework. You've got this!

ADVICE FROM . . . HOLLY GABRIELLE

Hey everyone, I'm Holly, or Holly Gabrielle in the world of social media. After spending three years at the University of Cambridge studying Biological Natural Sciences, which included intense three-hour exams supervised by professors in gowns and five days of back-to-back finals, optimising my revision had to be a priority. Whilst I started developing this system in school, which helped me reach my all A* grades at GCSE and A level, I only found this key three-step process as an undergraduate biologist.

Step 1: Identify your knowledge gaps

Any efficient revision strategy should always involve highlighting your weak points and what you don't already know. I usually do this by scribbling down anything and everything that I can remember from a particular topic, on plain or scrap paper (trust me, it's not going to be a framed piece of artwork) and then I'll compare this to my study notes to track down the missing pieces of the jigsaw. This is an example of blurting.

Step 2: Flashcards

"What do I write on a flashcard?" is a very commonly asked question when it comes to revising, but here's my solution: transfer only your knowledge gaps to a carefully crafted pile of flashcards. Write the question or prompt on the front and answer on the back. Problem solved.

Step 3: Summary sheets

At the apex of my revision funnel I'll create a summary sheet on plain A4 paper, and this is what I'll be using to revise from just before an exam; this is dedicated to only the information that I simply struggle to remember. Attempting to go over everything you've learned the night before an exam is neither a healthy goal nor manageable task, and so this is why I find summary sheets to be immensely powerful.

These methods work incredibly well for me and I'd perhaps even go as far as saying I love the process! The repetition and rigour of revision takes discipline, but I know it's always worth it in the end. Whilst my system may be something you'd like to try, I encourage you to discover one that works best for you. Finding revision techniques that allow you to achieve your best results will also take time, so don't be scared to get creative and do a bit of experimenting as you journey through your studies!

Good luck and keep smiling, you're doing an amazing job!

CHAPTER 5

IT'S TIME FOR TIMETABLES

8:00pm	*Revise chemistry*
8:02pm	*Mental breakdown*
8:03pm	**Try to pull myself together**
8:04pm	*Flick through notes. Or Instagram.*
8:05pm	*Call it a day. I worked too hard.*

I was raised on my dad asking me, 'What are the five Ps of success?' To which I would groan, roll my eyes and pretend that those five words hadn't become ingrained in my skull over the last two decades.

'Perfect planning prevents poor performance.' Ah yes, the five words which are so easy to understand, yet so hard to internalise. Welcome to chapter 5 – the key to unlocking productivity through planning.

This chapter will help you to establish an effective study routine, set achievable study goals and hold yourself accountable for your deadlines. Whether you're a long-term planner or a night-before crammer, knowing how to timetable your life is an essential skill for when you need to power through your work.

When I was doing my GCSEs, I had 12 different subjects. That's 5 lessons a day, 150+ modules, 24 exams. The thought of revising for that made me shudder. It still does. No, thank you.

I was first introduced to the idea of study timetables by my good friend Ruby Granger. A fellow YouTuber in the space of studying and productivity, Ruby is incredibly effective at managing her time.

Timetabling is the cure that stops you thinking about work and start doing it. It invites you to prioritise, create a high-level plan for your life based on deadlines and assign appropriate lengths of time to each task until they're all done. It's a way of making 24 exams feel (slightly more) manageable and empowers you to spend your time well.

One of the key secrets here is practice. The more often you plan your time, the better you get at estimating how long tasks take you.

Maybe the thought of timetabling makes you shudder. I know I had tried it before, felt the stress of not having completed everything on my list and subsequently abandoned the plan every day thereafter. But when I collated advice from tens of top students at GCSE and A level, I found all of them had a revision timetable of some kind.

First, we'll review how to go about creating a study timetable, then we'll review some of the classic do's and don'ts and look at how to transform a list of tasks into an effective plan. The process of timetabling has three main guiding forces: the urgency of each topic in terms of your current level of understanding, the urgency of action based on upcoming deadlines and, finally, balance. It is so important to be mindful of your mental health, scheduling sufficient breaks and making time for social activities. Here are the questions you should be asking yourself for each stage:

Urgency of understanding
What are my priority topics to revise?
How will I tackle them?

Urgency of deadline
When is my exam?
When do I need to submit this homework?

Balance
How can I schedule sufficient breaks and be
mindful of other important activities?

It's easy to read this chapter, nod at the words and feel like it makes sense. However, timetabling takes practice (and learning from inevitable failure). Even if it's not currently exam season, I dare you to create a revision schedule for tomorrow after reading this chapter. The earlier you can master this habit, the more it'll help you when stressful times hit!

1. WHAT ARE YOUR PRIORITY AREAS?

There is a famous quote from Peter Drucker, a business leader, which says, 'If you cannot measure it, you cannot improve it.' All the topics you need to revise are a scattered web in your mind; without detailing each one and quantifying your progress, you cannot actively improve how you tackle them.

Are there certain subjects where you need to achieve a certain grade to progress into what you plan to do next? Or is there one area that stands out as needing some work? For example, did your recent end of chapter test reveal that you are *tragic* at French? Be honest with yourself as it is the only way you'll be able to effectively timetable your subjects. You have a limited amount of time before exams, and it's important to allocate it efficiently.

Before you can start timetabling, you need to understand what you don't know. If I can name every song on the UK Top 50 charts and reasonably tell you how well I know the lyrics, then why can't I tell you how well I know my subjects? The best way to do this is to rank your understanding of every little topic.

In the Easter holidays before my GCSE exams, I wrote a list of every topic in every subject in an Excel spreadsheet. Yep, all of them. I went on the exam boards' websites for every subject I was taking to make sure I had the right information. Initially, this was overwhelming. I stared at the seemingly endless list as though starting secondary school anew. However, I then colour-coded each one based on how strong I felt on the content. Instantly, I started discarding topics that did not need my attention. If I could go through a flashcard set with ease, this topic was not worth deep practice. I focused on areas I didn't understand or had performed poorly in.

Don't be generous. If you don't understand a topic, brutally mark it with urgency, whether you enjoy revising it or not. I had a simple traffic light system of green, amber and red. Green meant it needed very little attention, amber required moderate revision and dark red was a problem point which begged more time. I then added a new column to my spreadsheet: Actions. In this, I detailed the strategies I intended to use to get my problem areas to green, using SAAD techniques like flashcard sets and past papers. Telling myself what I would do revealed to me where I did not have sufficient resources. Had I made flashcards for that topic yet? Did I understand the content or would I need to see a teacher?

Be honest with yourself and don't skip this phase! You can't create a plan without first knowing where to direct your energy.

I also added a simple 'Last Reviewed' and 'Next Review' section to aid my spaced repetition process (flick back to chapter 3 for a refresh of this!). Knowing when I last revised certain concepts was incredibly helpful in planning effective future revision. Here's an example of what the prioritisation process looked like:

Topic	Urgency	Actions	Notes	Last Reviewed	Next Review
Chapter 11 – Photosynthesis		Flashcards and blurting	Need to make flashcards!	13/01/18	18/01/18
Chapter 12 – Respiration		Object association; Do specific exam-style questions		02/01/18	20/02/18

(Continued)

Chapter 13 – Ecosystem		Do specific exam-style questions		14/12/17	25/02/18
Chapter 14 – Stimuli		Blurting, flashcard set and past paper questions	Ask teacher for past paper questions	28/12/17	01/02/18
Chapter 15 – Nervous Coordination and Muscles		Blurting, flashcard set and past paper questions		14/12/17	16/01/18
Chapter 16 – Homeostasis		Go see teacher	Got a C in end of chapter test	N/A – go revise	19/01/18

2. DRAFT UP A TIMETABLE

There are a range of different tools you can use to create timetables. There are calendar functions on Notion, which is a website and app that helps you get organised, and study apps like My Study Life; you can drop tasks directly into your Google calendar or, of course, use pen and paper in a notebook or bullet journal.

I went through most of secondary school only using paper timetables and Excel spreadsheets but I've fallen in love with my Google calendar and Notion setup at university. Whatever works for you is best. Experiment, try out a few things, but, most importantly, *start*.

How detailed you make the table is up to you. I recommend having a time-to-time setup as the first column so that you can get specific with how long tasks will take you. Scheduling an event from 7:15pm–8pm is more realistic than simply writing 'complete this evening'.

3. WHAT ELSE IS GOING ON IN YOUR LIFE?

Fill in any mandatory extracurricular activities, events or classes for the week. I blocked off time for school, school activities and social activities. Colour coding is useful to see how you are dividing your time. For example, if sports practice is green, breaks are yellow and revision sessions are red, you can see if you are incorporating a good balance of breaks with just one glance. Are you spending sufficient time relaxing and socialising? When can you find stress-free time to revise?

4. WHEN DO YOU WORK BEST?

Call me crazy, but early mornings are my thing. If I wanted to work most optimally, it meant getting up at 5 or 6am and studying with deep focus for a few hours before school. Everyone is different but there are always times in the day that are less optimal. For example, the post-lunch afternoon slump is a real phenomenon for many, so you might not power through an essay at 2pm. Studies suggest that early mornings bring enhanced clarity. In planning your study sessions in advance, you can commit to an early night beforehand and get ready to smash the next day.

Whenever you work best, position your most important tasks at those times. Let's just say, if I had tried to write my homework essays at 2am, my teacher would have ended up reading gibberish. I am proudly not a night owl. Early birds unite.

5. STICK TO THE TIMETABLE AS BEST YOU CAN BUT ADAPT IT AS YOU PRACTISE

Especially at the start, timetables should be flexible. Did going over those flashcards take you 15 minutes as planned, or 45 minutes? Note that down for next time to help with your planning.

THE PLANNING FALLACY

If you're still struggling to estimate how long things are taking you, don't stress. It turns out that us humans are pretty bad at predicting how long things take us because we have a tendency to underestimate tasks and overvalue our abilities. This is called the planning fallacy. It's an optimistic bias towards thinking things take less time than they do.

One trick to help you create better estimates for future timetables is what personal development blogger Steve Pavlina coined, The Fudge Ratio. It takes into account the planning fallacy and gives you a numerical value to make better predictions:

1. Write down everything you need to do.
2. Estimate how long each task will take you. Don't think too much, just guess.
3. Complete the tasks while timing how long they take you. Write down this exact number.

4. Divide this actual task time by your estimate. This is your personal Fudge Ratio.

For example, I always underestimated how long it would take me to write flashcards. I would write down my estimate – a confident 10 minutes – to create the whole deck for a topic. In reality, it took me 30 minutes. Using basic maths (aka a few lazy taps on my phone calculator app), I would determine my Fudge Ratio as 30 minutes / 10 minutes = 3. Now I know that for a similar task of writing flashcards, I should probably multiply whatever my intuitive estimate is by 3. Eventually, you develop a new, more accurate intuition. You'll have a better understanding of how long tasks actually take you and be able to make more actionable timetables.

THE DON'TS OF TIMETABLING

Here are the many, many mistakes I made in my timetabling journey, so that you don't have to! This section is a game of, 'Spot the Mistake'. Take a look at each timetable and try to guess the fundamental flaw. When you make your next study plan, come back to this list and double check you're not falling prey to these simple pitfalls. May the timetabling be with you!

Time-to-time scheduling without 'shuffling time' in between

| 7:15am–7:25am | Go over chapter 5 computer science flashcards |
| 7:25am–7:45am | Write an essay plan for English literature homework |

Have a look at the snapshot of one of my old study timetables above. Can you see what the issue is?

This appears to be a clear plan, especially because I took the time to focus on priority subjects *and* do it at a time I would be most effective. However, the timings are continuous. I am going straight from one task at 7:25am to another at the same time. I have not left any time in between these activities. If I am revising computer science, there is no way my flashcards will magically put themselves away and be replaced by an English literature essay as the clock strikes 7:25am.

In reality, you need 'shuffling' time – a.k.a. that dead two-to-five minutes when you put your books away, take a sip of water and find your next round of revision notes.

All I needed to do to make this timetable successful was to start my next task at 7:30am instead of 7:25am. By affording myself five minutes between tasks, I'm leaving myself room for the first task to run a little bit over and time to shuffle the next study activity into place.

Too rigid

| 8:30pm–8:37pm | Complete five pages of maths homework for tomorrow's class |
| 8:40pm–8:50pm | Research Picasso's painting 'Guernica' and write down my interpretation |

Yet another deceptive example.

This time, I did my best. I knew it would be a productive day. I was full of optimism and good study energy. Even though I knew that my maths homework would take me at least 15 minutes, surely with the pressure of my 100+ task to-do list, I could get it done in 7?

Welcome to the fallacy of optimism.

Until you know how long it *really* takes you to get things done, be pessimistic. Always schedule more time than you know you need for a task. If you think it'll take between 10 and 15 minutes, be generous. Give it 20.

There is no better feeling than being ahead on your timetable and the only way you can achieve this is by being more realistic with your timings.

Too vague

9:00pm–9:25pm	Revise history
9:30pm–9:50pm	Learn more Spanish

Now this one is obvious. And yet this is a mistake I make to this day.

Imagine how overwhelmed I was when I settled into my desk, ready to slay my revision, only for my timetable to tell me that I needed to 'revise history'. What did I mean? Was I to sit and revise every account of every world war, coronation and international treaty?

It is tempting not to plan the specifics of your revision because that takes time and energy. While it is a good idea to make an overview of your week with time blocked off for certain subjects, the way to make your timetable most helpful is by specifying which area of a subject you are going to tackle. Which modules do you feel less comfortable with? What type of revision method would help you here? Make sure your revision is a little less sad and a lot more SAAD! The more you think about the specifics of a task in advance, the less friction there is to just starting. So invest the time in making your timetable specific.

Giving up on the timetable when you miss one task

10:00pm–10:25pm	Blurt organic chemistry mechanisms in chapter 3
10:30pm–10:45pm	Go over Quizlet set for new Spanish vocab
10:50pm–10:55pm	*abandoned*

If you're a perfectionist like me, this might be tough to hear. Brace yourself.

You are never going to stick to your timetable perfectly.

There will always be tasks which run over, concepts you thought you understood but don't or even surprise events which mean you can't do any of that night's planned revision.

That's okay.

Missing the odd task doesn't say anything about you. What does say something about you is what you choose to do next.

If you've missed two or three tasks, do you decide to abandon the whole timetable from now on and watch Netflix? If you've failed once, you'll likely fail again, right?

It's surprising that a productivity tool which was meant to bring me so much ease actually started making me more stressed. The idea of not sticking to my plan brought up feelings of low self-worth, hopelessness and a monumental fear of failure. When you treat your timetable like the holy grail, you are destined to fail.

What I had to learn was while it might feel like the timetable dictates your life, *you* dictate the timetable. If you need to change something around, move a task to the next day or scribble out this evening's plans and start afresh, go for it. Don't be as perfectionistic as 16-year-old Jade and think that one loss on your timetable has to impact the whole day.

Check in with your plan. Notice where you're at. Reshuffle. Learn from it.

Not scheduling breaks and other life activities

The final don't is all about hustling too hard. We've somehow been taught along our school career that the longer we spend revising, the better. In reality, it's meaningful breaks that allow us to spend time more productively.

Just like you schedule your revision tasks, make sure to schedule dedicated time to relax.

THE DO'S OF TIMETABLING

I'm sure by now you can guess some of the do's.

- DO give yourself breaks.
- DO make your timetable flexible and generous.
- DO adapt your timetable as you go on. Stick with it even if you miss the odd task.
- DO make your timetable based on priority subjects and modules.
- DO plan tasks at the times of the day you are most effective.

I'll never admit it, but my dad was right. Planning does prevent poor performance – and stress.

Before you move onto chapter 6, make this chapter meaningful. Get out a pen and paper, a trusty notebook or use a study app and make yourself a timetable for tomorrow. Factor in when you have school and other commitments, identify what you want to get done and see how effective you can be when you plan these activities into your day.

Every minute invested smartly now is a gift to Future You. Imagine flicking open that exam paper and seeing a question you practised just last week.

Time is currency. How will you choose to invest yours?

PUT IT IN PRACTICE:

- Create a timetable for a study session tomorrow.
- Check back though the Do's and Don'ts to make sure it's the best timetable possible and that you're not falling into any common traps.
- Use your timetable and note down if tasks take you longer than expected. Estimation takes practice!

ADVICE FROM . . . EVE BENNETT

After achieving all A*s in both her GCSEs and A levels, Eve is currently studying German and Spanish at the University of Oxford. She was one of the pioneers of StudyTube and is well-known for her colourful wall of Post-it notes, time-management skills and advocacy of mental health.

Planning is not only vital to maximise the time you have, but also to ensure you don't spend every waking hour slumped miserably over your desk. Good timetabling can allow you to get in all the revision you need, but also leaves time for socialising, exercise, relaxation and for all the hobbies and interests that make you *you*! What's the point in spending 12+ hours sat at your desk, missing out on plans and stuck in a limbo where you're not focused but not relaxed either?

What really helped me during exam season was dividing up all my time commitments/priorities into different coloured blocks. For example, revision would be green, rest time would be blue, extracurricular activities would be yellow and plans with friends would be purple. I would then make a grid dividing each day over the week into hour blocks (or 30 minute segments if you prefer) on a spreadsheet.

I'd start by filling in the things that are at fixed times such as dance classes, driving lessons, study sessions in school, etc. I then decided how much time I would like to commit to studying each day (this varied depending on the day of the week and how close I was to sitting the exam) and started to fill in the spreadsheet, making sure to add in regular breaks.

I personally know I prefer to get up early and get my focussed hours of revision out of the way, but if you're a night owl then the beauty of a timetable is that you can fill it out to suit your individual needs! The time blocks also allow you to schedule your breaks at intervals that work best for you – I know some people who like a smaller break every 30 minutes, whilst others prefer a hefty break after a couple of hours.

It's incredibly important to make sure you take at least one day each week with either less 'blocks' allocated for revision, or none at all – social activities and self-care time are equally as important and should be a top priority when you're scheduling your time. Also, don't be afraid to be flexible – if something comes up, move blocks to different days or delete them altogether and start again tomorrow!

Learning to schedule your time in a way that is not restrictive but also allows you to get more out of the precious time you have is an incredibly useful skill. It helped me stay sane amidst the craziness of exam season, and I guarantee you'll notice a difference if you start to structure your time more!

CHAPTER 6

PRODUCTIVITY HACKS

You only have to turn to YouTube to see that productivity is everywhere.

'Productive Day in the Life.'

'12-Hour Productive Study with Me.'

'How to Never Procrastinate and Always Be Productive.'

I'm guilty of it too. The buzzword 'productivity' exploded through online spaces like gossip in the classroom to the point where its meaning was lost. We operate in an achievement-based hustle culture where we often value work with tangible output more than we value fostering relationships or relaxation. Think about it: there is no grand award for cooking yourself dinner. There is no promise of a better future when we decide to Face-Time our friends. There is no seal of approval from chilling with your phone. In our pursuit of what brings perceived validation, it is easy to glamorise looooong hours of studying under the excuse of a productive day or feel extreme guilt for breaking an unrealistic study schedule.

What does productivity even really mean?

Maybe the first image that pops into your mind is someone sitting at their desk for ten hours, studying to the brink of insanity. But in reality, productivity just means **spending your time well**. It's about optimising your hours to do everything you love in a meaningful way. It's about getting the work done efficiently so you actually have *more* time to spend with friends, watching shows or going on adventures. To me, that's productivity. Not doing more, but doing what needs to be done. Time well spent.

I define productivity as, 'focusing on what is really important at a moment in time, with intentionality'.

Does that mean that binge-watching your favourite show is productive? Yes. As long as you are doing it with intention, it is time well spent!

Relaxing is productive. Learning is productive. Hanging out with friends is productive. Heck, even playing video games until 4am just to unlock that last level is productive. If you can optimise the time you spend on tasks you *don't* want to do, you'll have more time to spend on those you *do*. The more productively you can study, the more you'll embrace your time spent on other things too.

The origins of productivity date back to the industrial era where being productive meant producing the most goods in the shortest amount of time. Factory workers had to assemble products in the most efficient way to maximise output. From this, we can generate the equation:

Productivity = Output / Time

But we're not machines. Productivity doesn't necessarily mean creating a physical good, but rather optimising for a chosen output which is meaningful to you based on your priorities. When prioritising the outcome of relaxation, we are looking for activities which create this in the allotted time given. During revision sessions, we are always optimising for the **most knowledge acquired** or the **deepest understanding possible** using the **least amount of time**. This is how you are being most productive and spending your time in the best way.

So, to increase productivity and maximise knowledge retention, we can either increase the quality of our knowledge retention or decrease the time it takes to get there.

Increase Quality of Output: The 3 Fs

To increase the quality of useful output from study sessions, you must maximise the 3 Fs: Focus, Forethought and Fun. These three concepts directly impact your ability to get the most out of your revision.

The first F to increase the quality of the output is to enhance your **Focus**.

$$\text{Productivity} = \frac{\text{Output}}{\text{Time}} \times \text{Focus}$$

- Focus = lack of distractions, such as studying in a quiet place. It is about finding a flow where your brain is engaged without deviation. Flow is defined as an engrossing state where deep work is taking place. We all know the feeling of being halfway through a maths problem when everything seems to fade away as we calculate.
- But focus is also as simple as being intentional with one task at a time. Yep, one. Rather than flitting between tasks to eventually generate 'output', being truly productive means giving each task the mental space it deserves. Maintaining focus

on just one task not only reduces the time taken but adds a new level of enjoyment because you feel less stressed. The task is being done deliberately, with dedicated time just for its completion. You maximise the quality of the output when intentional mental power is directed to it.

The second F to increase your quality of work is **Forethought**.

$$\textbf{Productivity} = \frac{\textbf{Output}}{\textbf{Time}} \times \textbf{Focus} \times \textbf{Forethought}$$

- With hundreds of tasks at hand, planning is essential. Even taking five minutes in the morning to plan your day's activities gives your revision direction. Your study session will be of a higher quality when you have planned what to cover. This also helps reduce the time spent studying through minimising friction to starting.

And finally, as my good friend and YouTuber Ali Abdaal often says, you are more productive when you are having Fun.

$$\textbf{Productivity} = \frac{\textbf{Output}}{\textbf{Time}} \times \textbf{Focus} \times \textbf{Forethought} \times \textbf{Fun}$$

When you are enjoying what you are learning, you are more likely to take it in and show up to the next study session. Time is being spent doubly well as you are maximising the output of knowledge retention *and* overall happiness.

This chapter will dig into productivity hacks to maximise the 3 Fs (Focus, Forethought and Fun) when studying. To reduce the time taken to complete tasks, we will also look at techniques to tackle the bane of our lives – procrastination.

Of course, being productive is easier said than done. Most of us are not truly productive – just busy. It's human nature not to be aware of our priorities and to just go along with where the day takes us, even if it means we end up with less time for the things we love doing.

Without robust habits to optimise study time, it is easy to fall into what I like to call 'half-revising'. Pretending to revise. Looking occasionally at your phone. Sort of doing 7,364,930 other tasks while 'studying'. Multi-tasking feels gratifying. It's reading one page of geography notes and then scrolling for five minutes on TikTok. If the textbook is out, you feel like a productive super-hero. Really, you're just avoiding deep focus. And half-revising is stressful because you never dedicate yourself to one thing. If you're not meant to be on your phone at that moment, you can't enjoy it in the same way. You feel an underlying guilt that you are bypassing a more pressing task.

And just because you are revising doesn't mean you are doing good revision. When you are staring at flashcards but your mind is elsewhere, you are decreasing the useful output from that task *and* dragging it out so it takes up unnecessary time. So how do you get intentional? How do you find focus? How can you achieve productivity in your study life so that you truly spend time well on activities which matter most to you?

To answer these questions, we need to dig into our distractions, commitments and, of course, our dreaded enemy ... procrastination. In this chapter, let's stop trying to be 'busy' for the sake of *doing*. Let's start getting productive.

NEVER STARTING SYNDROME

The groan that filled the Year 10 geography classroom as the teacher squeaked her dying pen across the board was so loud, I was sure even the Year 7s could hear us:

End of chapter test: Monday.

Perfect. Amazing. Brilliant. What had been a mediocre, maybe even lovely, Friday was now ruined.

Between the unhappy murmurs of people around me, I pulled out my planner and unenthusiastically flicked to that week. I found the dreaded day and wrote a sad, non-committal 'Geography test'. In the precious blank space where my weekend would be, I wrote an even sadder word: 'Revise'.

The rest of the lesson was clouded by the promise of Monday's test. We all knew this test mattered, even if the teacher said it didn't. We were nearing the end of the year and our predicted grades were being calculated. Parents' evening was round the corner, as were report cards. Pressure was mounting, as it always was.

'I'm not going to revise,' the girl next to me proudly proclaimed. 'I'm going to test my existing knowledge, you know? See what I need to revise in the future.'

Classic. I'd heard that one before. I'd even said that one before. We all know that when 'the future' comes, we want to revise even *less* than we do now.

'Are you sure you'll want to make flashcards in the Easter holidays though? It might be a bit late?'

'Nah, I'll be fine. By then I'll have to do it, you know?'

As the lesson went on, I counted the number of pages in the chapter we would be tested on. You know, just to torture myself.

Twenty-eight. Horrible. I was behind on notes. I'd missed a few lessons. I hadn't made a single flashcard. When the school bell rang and I trudged to the bus stop, the thought of revision suddenly felt overwhelming.

That Friday night, everything was interesting. Except for revision.

I had never been so busy. It suddenly felt like the perfect time to try out a new cake recipe. I was a gem of a daughter, helping my mum cook dinner and wash dishes. My younger brother was doing homework – and of course, I offered to help him. I folded and re-folded the clothes in my drawers. I scrolled through productivity videos on social media, certain that absorbing this life-changing information would somehow help me revise. When it finally came to the late evening and I settled at my desk, I was proud of my busyness.

'Yeah, I'll revise tomorrow instead,' I told myself.

The next day, all I saw was my phone dangling in my fingers, tapping away at every social media until my clock chimed another hour.

'I'll revise at 11:00am,' I told myself. Only for 11am to come and for 11:30am to suddenly look much more attractive. Because you have to start revision on round hours, obviously.

Isn't it funny how social media feels *that* much more enticing when you use it to avoid something you don't want to do? Conversations with old friends are suddenly juicy, desirable and necessary. That email you never wanted to reply to suddenly feels like life-or-death if you don't. You can't ignore your messy room, calling at you to clean it right now.

The most wonderful (and evil!) part of procrastination is that we mask it in a veil of productivity. Sure, cleaning my room gave me mental space. And yes, that three-hour FaceTime call with my best friend was necessary and fun. But in convincing ourselves that the little to-do list items are worth more than the high-effort, mentally taxing tasks, we are not practising productivity but avoidance. *This* is why we feel guilty when we don't do schoolwork. It's not about choosing between relaxing or doing work, it's about putting off things you need to do and not planning dedicated time for them in your calendar. If you know for certain the task will be done, then doing other things like calling friends or watching Netflix are not only acceptable, but productive too.

When another 'tomorrow' came, I surprisingly still didn't feel inspired to revise. I half-heartedly picked up my geography text-book – and an old season of *Gossip Girl* – until I was inspired to do something more challenging like Blurting, which requires active recall.

When I finally started to revise, I convinced myself that spending one Netflix season-worth of time *looking at geography* was more powerful than studying it deeply for half an hour. I didn't use SAAD revision techniques with desirable difficulty, nor active recall. Instead, I hoped for information-osmosis – or magic. This comes back to the idea of 'half-revising' and how we accept it under misconceptions of what it means to be productive. It took me time to realise that the quicker I completed my revision, the more time I could spend truly enjoying my life.

I wish I could have told myself then to stop waiting for inspiration. Stop waiting for motivation. Stop waiting until you 'feel like' doing something. Revision won't magically become fun until you dedicate meaningful effort to doing it well. Motivation is fleeting and unreliable, whereas habits and timetables reduce friction. Even when there's nothing you'd rather do less.

When I look back at how I approached revision for that end of chapter test, I see two main flaws:

Firstly, putting off deep work.

Secondly, pretending to do deep work.

And I also hyped up the dreaded revision so much that it became a barrier to starting. Twenty-eight pages of revision? No flashcards pre-made? What a nightmare.

Thinking about the work is always worse than just doing it.

Here are some of my all-time favourite hacks that changed my ability to be productive. I now use these frameworks every time I need to get something done, whether it's university work, YouTube projects or job applications. They help me focus on the task, find flow and ultimately enjoy the task more because I have committed to it. Then when I watch *Gossip Girl* or FaceTime my friends, I can commit to that too because I have done what I needed to do without spending all day on it.

So let's talk specific strategies to break down tasks into chunks that feel less intimidating, help us commit to doing the work deeply and, of course, tackle procrastination. Because 30 minutes of truly focused revision is worth more than a whole day of looking at a textbook half-heartedly. Goodbye Instagram. Hello airplane mode.

POMODORO TECHNIQUE

Welcome to the best productivity hack I've ever found: the Pomodoro Technique. I was first introduced to this by Thomas Frank's YouTube channel many years ago and it changed the way I approach work.

This technique uses a timer to help you break down your work into manageable 25-minute chunks separated by short breaks. It was developed by Francesco Cirillo in the late 1980s – he named it *pomodoro* – the Italian for tomato – after a tomato-shaped kitchen timer he used as a university student.

Here's how it works:

1. Choose a specific task, such as 'Complete five test questions from chapter 5'.
2. Set a 25-minute timer.
3. Spend those 25 minutes focused exclusively on the task you set. If you get distracted or stop working, you start the timer again. From the beginning.
4. After 25 minutes, reward yourself with a five-minute break.
5. Choose another task and repeat.

Each 25-minute segment or 'Pomodoro' forces you to get in the zone and direct your energy towards one task. Rather than flitting between topics, being half on your phone or tackling a task that is too general to meaningfully complete, the Pomodoro Technique simplifies the process in an efficient way. The idea is that by focusing on nothing but the task at hand and knowing you'll get a short break soon, you enter a much more productive frame of mind.

A little ode to me and my brain: I am a gross overthinker. My brain takes anything and extrapolates it in a hundred different ways. I imagine all the outcomes of different choices. More than anything, I make the *thought* of work harder than *doing* the actual work itself. Imagining the stress and effort required to complete tasks cripples me and stops me even starting.

Hence, the Pomodoro Technique reduces all friction to just starting. You don't need to finish all your revision in 25 minutes.

You just have to start. Once I've gotten into the frame of mind to focus, I often want to continue working even after the 25-minute timer goes off. That's the magic of forcing yourself to focus.

If you're reading this and you know you're putting something off, I dare you to start a 25-minute timer on your phone and just start. Dedicate time to that task and that task only.

Odds are, the hardest part of it all was just starting.

MONTHLY OVERVIEWS AND WEEKLY PLANS
(FORETHOUGHT)

If there's something which anchors productivity, it's a deep understanding of your priorities. It's true, you need to clean your room. And, ah yes, you promised you'd write that email. Throw in household chores, homework deadlines and a few exams to revise for, and suddenly you're looking at a mess of tasks.

How can you know what to prioritise if you don't make the time to evaluate your options?

Inspired by bullet journals, a few years ago I began making different plans to live my life by. These plans are the root of my ability to be productive. They guide my time and help me plan my days, and I feel less stressed because nothing can creep up on me. It's all there just waiting to be done.

Let's talk about a high-level month overview.

I begin by brainstorming everything I want to get done that month, answering this from the perspective of academic, health, social and personal goals. What do I want to feel like? How do I want to be? Are there any specific things I want to explore? What do I want to learn for fun? Do I have exams coming up? Friends' birthdays? I flick through my calendar and focus on everything that holds meaning.

Nowadays, I do this via the free productivity app Notion but you can do this in a journal, on paper or with a calendar app.

Once you've brainstormed the high-level outcomes you want from the month, start outlining more tangible goals that follow from this. For example, if your desired feeling is to have a more confident knowledge of a mathematical concept, your tangible goal might be to complete all the textbook questions and watch a series of videos on it.

Here's an example of a monthly and weekly plan:

March Overview

March priorities
- [ ] Improve my understanding of A Level chemistry
- [ ] Get better at integration (maths)
- [ ] Get more that 8 hours of sleep every night (!)
- [ ] Finish Coursera Accounting course
- [ ] Practise Blurting
- [ ] Make all flashcard sets for English lit quotes

Week 1 (3rd-9th)
- [ ] Go over Chem Test with Mrs McC.
- [ ] Complete all Qs in CGP maths book
- [ ] Blurt every day (bio + chem)
- [ ] Reread Wuthering Heights + bookmark good quotes
- [ ] Create sleep habit tracker

Week 2 (10th-16th)
Note: chem + English text this week!
- [ ] Make flashcards for characters
- [ ] Make all flashcards for themes
- [ ] Write practice essay for English lit
- [ ] Complete Chaps 8, 9 and 10 chem Qs
- [ ] Blurt chem knowledge

Week 3 (17th-23rd)
- [ ] Complete Week 2 of Accounting
- [ ] Complete Week 3 of Accounting
- [ ] Complete Week 4 of Accounting
- [ ] Edit vid on Blurting

Week 4 (24th-30th)
YouTube
- [ ] Complete past paper Qs on integration
- [ ] Blurt all chem Chap 8
- [ ] Go on after school session w Mrs McC

So you've got your high-level monthly goals. Time to plan your week.

Break down each high-level tangible goal into smaller, more manageable weekly goals that you can slot into your calendar. Let's take the example of improving your maths skills again. You might schedule an after-school session with your maths teacher in the first week, complete a page of textbook questions in the second week, which leads up to a mini test in the final week of the month.

From here, you start to detail your weekly outlines. These will be your anchors for planning your week. I review my weekly overview every Sunday or early Monday morning and use it to carve out how I want to spend my time.

School is bloody stressful and living day-to-day with no roadmap of where you're going only makes it worse. Having a feeling of control over the many things you have to do is not only helpful, but empowering. Through setting monthly goals, reviewing what worked well (and what didn't!) for last month and setting clear priorities, you can make sure you're giving yourself a good academic foundation *and* the space to just have fun.

This process is the reason I was able to juggle goals in many different realms of life. I started my YouTube channel during the most stressful years of sixth form, applied for internships, completed UCAS forms, became head girl of my school and ran the school council, all while making my top priority my mental health. However, there is no way I could have balanced these things (or remained a functioning human!) if not for planning.

That's what worked for me. Though it doesn't need to be as strict as a monthly or weekly plan. You need to try out some options to learn what's right for you. Maybe that's daily to-do lists or writing deadlines and important dates on a calendar in your room. Whatever it is, give some structure to the fast-flowing days of secondary school. Not only is it an incredible habit to develop for future life but it'll give you peace of mind, I promise.

TO-DO LISTS
(FORETHOUGHT)

This section has been on my to-do list for days. How ironic.

To-do lists are one of the easiest tools to use to understand what needs to be completed and prompt yourself to just do it. But what's the secret to a good to-do list? While you might want to make it look beautiful, the robustness of a to-do list is in its feasibility and prioritisation. We must ask ourselves what deserves to be on that list, especially because we gain validation from the act of crossing off items.

In building to-do lists, you have a choice:

- Fill your to-do list with the simplest tasks. This means they are easier to complete, which can serve as useful motivation. However, this may mean you end up avoiding larger, more difficult tasks because it will take longer to get the same buzz from ticking them off.
- Adopt a system of prioritisation where you rank tasks based on both their difficulty *and* their urgency. Change the extent of validation you gain from completing tasks based on whether or not they are most necessary.

My to-do listing process is built on the latter. It is about knowing every task I need to complete, yes. But even more importantly, I recognise that tasks aren't equal. For example, just because learning that TikTok dance is on your list, does it mean it's your *top* priority?

Over secondary school, I developed three simple steps to creating to-do lists . . . that actually get done.

1. **Brain dump**. Write down every task you need to complete. Every thought that's causing you stress. All the scary deadlines keeping you up at night. Until they're physically written somewhere, these thoughts are heavy. In fact, they're paralysing. I recently spoke to Mike Williams, co-author of the book *Get Things Done: For Teens*, and one of the points we discussed is the mental fatigue we feel when we know we have a lot to do. We become scattered and unable to start anything because we are aware there is so much to be done. The thought of starting one task and missing something we're forgetting is terrifying. So before you start a single task, get clear on everything that needs to be done. Go crazy. Blurt it all down.

2. **Specify, select and prioritise**. The beautiful thing about having all your tasks in front of you is that you can then get clear on what needs to be done when. Scribble your deadlines next to tasks and rank them by urgency. A simple colour coding scheme is useful to help you get a handle on which tasks are most important. I like numbering them in order of importance.

    When we initially write every task down, we're probably not being specific enough. It's tempting to be general when you know you have deadlines, such as 'Revise geography'. You know you have a test. You know you need to revise. However, being too general creates friction to starting. Get specific with your tasks. For example, 'Revise geography chapter 2 flashcards'.

Next, write down roughly how long each task will take you. Be as realistic as possible. As discussed in chapter 3 with timetabling, you will get better at estimating this with practice.

3. But what use are to-do lists and plans if you make them and never stick to them? **Slot your tasks into your timetable, schedule or calendar.** The only way these things will get done is if you make time for them. Rather than stopping at the stage of identifying what you need to do, dare yourself to actually go do them.

I have a habit of slotting tasks roughly into my Google calendar for the day. This helps me see how realistic it is to complete everything I said I would and I can readjust my priorities if necessary.

To-do lists are a whole trust exercise with yourself. Forget therapy – this is a free way to learn about how you commit to things.

You need to build up a level of trust in yourself and the importance you place on self-set deadlines. Going back to your monthly goals, if you have decided that improving your maths skills is valuable to you, remember that. Write it down somewhere you can see it every day. Own it. It doesn't matter if your friends have different goals. It doesn't matter if things crop up during the weeks that weren't in your initial plan. You can learn that the tasks you've planned for yourself are rooted in your value systems. In honouring them, you honour yourself.

SAYING NO, MEANINGFULLY
(FOCUS)

I still struggle with this. I am the biggest yes-woman you will ever meet. I am well known for being spontaneous, finding random adventures and saying yes to every café meetup, extra curricular club and fun project I can feasibly cram into my calendar. But I do this at the detriment of my self-set goals.

The world often raises us to be people pleasers. We're taught to put other people's needs before our own. I can't count the number of times I've sacrificed what is best for me in the moment through wanting to help others. If I was asked by a younger student to mentor them in GCSE chemistry, I found it nearly impossible to say no, even when my calendar was full of extra projects already. I spent four years volunteering for an incredible disability charity called Sportsable and every time they needed help at extra events, I typed 'yes' without even thinking.

At what point do you stop giving yourself to others in order to focus on your own goals?

I think it's about recognising what is essential and what is not. The more tangibly you define your own priorities, the easier it is to stick to them. I am still working on this. Here's your proof.

Just last week, I was getting run down from university work. I had to write three essays in one week, complete seven classes – each with three hours of reading – write a proposal, do my internship work . . . Oh, the list goes on. In my fatigue, the good habits which make me the best version of myself started to slip. My eye bags were gucci, my skin was complaining about my quick-fix late-night snacks and my daily habit of exercise was compromised.

On paper, the workload was manageable. If I had kept my head down and remembered my priorities of physical and mental health, I would have planned these habits into my day and stuck to them. Instead, I started yet another project with a friend, watched Netflix with my roommates for hours, thus ignoring my deadline, and said yes to attending random events which did not create meaningful value. I don't even know why I said yes to them. I am the queen of FOMO.

Saying no is not about sacrificing enjoyment. It is not about rejecting spontaneity, which is beautiful and creates memorable experiences. **Learning to say no is about saying yes to yourself.** It is about honouring priorities you set for yourself in the past to benefit your future and sticking to them.

Saying no does not hurt other people. We have this bias towards thinking that all opportunities are fleeting and so saying no once means we will never have the chance again. We also inflate how much time there is in one week, mentally rearranging the less exciting habits like sleep and revision to find ways of making other events fit. When friendships get tangled in the equation of planning time, we also worry that choosing our own priorities over our friends' will harm these relationships. This is untrue. With good planning and an awareness of what you wish to achieve and when, you can make time for your goals *and* people in a meaningful way. When you choose to.

Whenever I find myself about to say yes to something that I probably shouldn't, I try to keep in mind that what I am really doing is saying no to something else.

What are you putting off? Which previous commitments are you ignoring? How are you compromising the things that keep you well and happy? Be mindful of these. And be willing to say no when you need to. I implore you.

High-density fun only

The opposite of being a yes-woman is the classic, "Oh, I'm sorry, I can't make it! I have too much revision to do." This is the kind of person who pulls out their phone two seconds later and spends the rest of the afternoon scrolling (guilty!).

Rather than making yourself feel better for rejecting social events in the pursuit of studying, commit to planning high-density fun. Prioritise that movie night, that sports session and trying out that new recipe. You're more likely to speed up the revision to go enjoy yourself.

Half-revising sucks. Match high-density revision with high-density fun!

RECOMMENDED APPS
(FORETHOUGHT, FOCUS AND FUN!)

Pen and paper did their best. We tried to hold a hundred commitments on scraps of paper or in our phone notes. I went through most of secondary school reliant only on my school planner. But if you're looking to level up your productivity system, I have a few recommendations for you. Heads up, I'm writing this in 2020 (what a year) but if you're sitting there in 2101 (oh my god, I hope you have cool holograms), these apps might be vintage tales of the past. Nonetheless, here they are:

Notion: I've mentioned it a few times because this desktop and phone app is my best friend. It has so many capabilities that it can feel initially overwhelming to learn how to use but when you do, it's life changing. I use this for planning, journaling, brainstorming and ideation. I write my class notes and timetables in Notion too!

Forrest: this phone app is the best for productive study sessions! Inspired by the Pomodoro Technique mentioned above, you can use your time spent studying to grow trees. If you touch your phone during the time set, your tree dies. I'm not sure there's a better way to teach you to focus and commit. If you can turn revision into a fun game (and avoid murdering a tree), it feels less of a chore.

Todoist: if you love to-do lists but find yourself haphazardly writing them in the notes section of your phone, this app will help you keep track of tasks in a centralised way. You get motivational messages as you complete tasks and the interface is highly intuitive.

Any **calendar** app: I slot most of my events into my Google calendar. While I think bullet journals and paper planners are so special, the added benefit of reminder notifications is very useful. I especially love the flexibility of rearranging my day when events change.

And there you have it! Procrastination who?

But seriously, these hacks are easy to read and much harder to do. I recommend you take the time to stop reading here, go back and assess where you're at in your own life. Do you make time for your own goals? Do you regularly plan? What do you need to help you use your time productively and make sure you can do all the things you want to do?

If you're reading this and you need a reason to go start your work, this is it. I'm sending productive energy from my keyboard to the ink of your very page. You are holding pure productivity in your fingers.

Go say yes to working for Future You. You've got this.

PUT IT IN PRACTICE:

- Choose a task you've been procrastinating about for *ages*. Put your phone away, start a 25-minute Pomodoro Timer and just do it. Commit to working only on that task for the whole 25 minutes and then give yourself a five-minute break. Odds are, you'll be inspired to continue!
- Make a high-level plan for your month, upcoming week and then a broken down to-do list for today. What do you need to get done? What are you putting off?

ADVICE FROM . . . RENEE KAPUKU

Renee is a content creator, entrepreneur and academic. She graduated from the University of Oxford with a first class in history, and graduated from Harvard University with honours in international education policy. She is an entrepreneur in residence at the New Entrepreneurs Foundation, co-founder of the Phoenix programme, founder of the Well Collective and co-founder of the ToMySisters talk show.

Procrastination always gets the best of us. It's gotten me, and chances are, it's had you at some point in your journey. Have you ever experienced the weird paradox of having so many things to do, that you end up doing nothing at all? As a former student, this was definitely my reality. I was juggling all my subjects, alongside my commitments to student societies, and all my other hobbies like sports and drama. Each week, I'd find myself super tired and burnt out – and yet, it still felt as though I wasn't really getting anything done. It still felt like I wasn't really making progress. Plus, I'd find myself in the same situation the following week where I'd have essays due . . . and things to do!

How did I learn to become super productive? Prioritisation. Often, when we compile a list of things that need to be done, the length of the list can be so overwhelming. But, the key to managing your work is prioritisation, not procrastination. This means you need to figure out what are the biggest, chunkiest and most important things you need to do each day, before knocking out the rest of your commitments.

I used to just write a pretty arbitrary list of things I needed to do, and then always found myself in a bit of a mess because, by the end of the day, I was actually doing the essay that probably should've been started a little bit earlier on in the day. Here's how you can put it into practise a bit more practically.

Write out your list of tasks for the week, and rank each according to the following:

1. Projected time and effort needed to complete the task
2. Time constraint and a deadline for task
3. Why this task matters in the grand scheme of your goals

Rank these on a scale of 1–5, 5 being the high amount of time and effort needed, most pressing deadline and most important in the context of your big-picture goals. Now, work through your list in the order of priorities. Once you knock out the top items, you'll find yourself breathing a lot easier as you've taken care of the most important things first!

CHAPTER 7

HOMEWORK HACKS

Every day, I took the bus home from school. Not just any bus, *the* bus. What was a forced commute to drag us home every day became the coolest hangout space – with a reputation. The bus was the gossip hub, a place to debrief our days and a space to interact with students from other schools.

It was a routine. Hear the end-of-school bell ring, slap our bags on our backs and practically sprint to the gate, breathlessly in anticipation of the lowdown on today's tea. What did that teacher say to you? How was the French exam? She did *what* at breaktime?

For 40 minutes, there was no work, no deadlines and no reason to remember why we wore matching school uniforms. The bus was ours.

Why do I bring this up?

Because the bus journey didn't last forever. The second I stepped off that bus and into my house, the last thing I wanted to do was get out my school books. After an exhausting day of lessons, the bus was a reminder of everything I *wanted* to be doing: socialising, chilling on my phone and travelling. I could still feel the ghost of a pen in my hand. And I didn't want to pick it up again.

But just as the bus became a routine, one which required little thought and little effort, and just as the bus went from a boring necessity to a part of my day I not only tolerated but enjoyed, so too could doing my homework become a pre-planned, easy and enjoyable part of my day.

Welcome to chapter 7: Homework Hacks.

We all have work to do. We all have exams to prepare for. But the good thing is, there are ways to make it easier to get all the things you don't want to do done. This chapter will make you feel like homework is easy, or at least tolerable!

ROUTINE, ROUTINE, ROUTINE

Choices are exhausting. When we get home, we're bombarded with them. Would we rather drink tea, or grab a juice? Should we wear pyjamas or normal clothes? Or even keep our school uniforms on? Most of all, do we really *want* to do homework? Or is Netflix calling you from the other room with its sweet, sweet promise of a good show?

The way to hack human psychology is to eliminate the feeling of choice. Rather than begging yourself every day to pick up your school planner, make it a pre-made arrangement by developing a routine. The beauty of routine is that it becomes automatic. You can train yourself to put your phone away and start making a to-do list.

Any routine is grounded in habits. To develop it takes hard commitment and discipline until it feels easy. I often relapsed into going on my phone straight after school, only to scramble to finish my work late at night. Every time you break routine, you're dishonouring the progress Past You made.

So what kind of routine do you want to have?

Whether you focus your schoolwork in after-school power sessions at home, attend homework clubs at school or structure your weekends to set up the school week, find what works for you around your other commitments and stick to it.

Let me take you through a typical day in my life after school.

After waving away my bus friends, my after-school experience began with the most fundamental hack of all: snacks. Something about a full day of school made me desperate for food. I got home around 3:45pm and until 4:15pm was my Snack and Chill Time. Nothing else.

In those luscious 30 minutes, I'd check in with my family, eat more snacks, and relax. I always tried to avoid social media as soon as I got home because the addictive quality of videos or scrolling would turn my 30 minutes into 60, or 180 (or 12 hours . . .).

Once I felt mildly more alive, the official power routine began. No matter how tired or unmotivated I felt, I'd put my phone away, sit down at my desk, pull out my school planner and Blurt down everything I knew I had to do. Cue my 'to-do list' process from chapter 6. I wrote down everything, from homework problem sheets for the next day and essay plans to revision and end of chapter tests. Any task on my mind went here too, even making thumbnails for YouTube videos. There's something cathartic about brain-dumping everything. When you hold all your tasks in your head, there's a constant anxiety that you might forget one or not sufficiently plan to complete it.

Brain-dumping is a stress reliever. Here's an example of mine:

- Do Mrs Saunders' homework sheet for tomorrow
- Revise chapter 7 of RS for test on Wednesday

- Email Miss Bassett about help on integration past paper Qs
- Make poster for geography on Friday
- Plan presentation for French club
- Start planning prefect speech for assembly

When I had all the tasks in front of me, I began to sort them by priority. For example, if I knew I had an end of chapter test the next day, my priority would be revision. I would then jot down roughly how long each task would take me, being as specific as possible.

1. Do Mrs Saunders' homework sheet for tomorrow (~**45 minutes**)
2. Revise chapter 7 of RS for test on Wednesday (~**2 hours**; blurting and flashcards)
3. Email Miss Bassett about help on integration past paper Qs (~**10 minutes**)
4. Make poster for geography on Friday (~**1 hour**)
5. Plan presentation for French club (~**1 hour**)
6. Start planning prefect speech for assembly (~**30 minutes**)

Then, without thinking, I'd allocate the next few hours to my tasks and slot the plan into my calendar. All of a sudden, the choice was made for me. There would be no painful shuffling of sheets or trying to work out what was a priority. I could just start.

4:30pm–5:15pm: Mrs Saunders' homework sheet
5:20pm–6:00pm: Anki flashcard set on RS chapter 7
6:00pm–6:30pm: Break for dinner
6:35pm–7:00pm: Blurt knowledge of RS chapter 7 and compare to notes

7:00pm–7:30pm: RS past paper Qs

7:30pm–8:00pm: Break

8:00pm–8:10pm: Email Miss Bassett

8:15pm–9:00pm: Listen to good music and make geography poster

Move to tomorrow after school:

Plan presentation for French club (~1 hour)

Start planning prefect speech for assembly (~30 minutes)*

Physically writing out tasks into a timed schedule makes you realise how realistic your to-do list is. Through prioritising tasks based on urgency, I can re-allocate less important tasks to the next day and have a deeper focus on those for today.

And just before I began working through my fresh to-do list, I'd write down something I was looking forward to that night. Selecting a reward early on is game-changing. Anything from watching an episode of my favourite TV show to calling a friend or watching a YouTube video. Suddenly, I had a very good reason to start, and finish, my work.

Perhaps you've heard of Parkinson's Law. **Work expands to fill the time you give it**. Rather than giving myself the whole evening to complete something, slotting it into a calendar and having a clear goal that night was the motivation I needed.

PROCRASTIN— OH LOOK, MY PHONE

Procrastination. The bane of our lives.

There's nothing quite like the power of an undesirable task to make other undesirable tasks suddenly seem essential. If you're reading this as a compulsive Instagram scroller, car-washer or hair-braider in times of heavy workloads, I relate.

This tip is borrowed from the last chapter but is worth mentioning here because it directly applies to homework. If you struggle to start working, make it a habit to complete one Pomodoro session every single day. The Pomodoro Technique is the best hack for meaningful, productive work as it functions like a 25-minute homework sprint of deep, focused work followed by a five-minute break to reward yourself. So if you're struggling to even begin your homework, this is a good place to start. Set a timer and commit to only focusing on one task for the duration. It takes so much more effort to start than it does to finish. Sprint. Sprint. Sprint.

But looking at the bigger picture – what causes procrastination? Distractions.

If you find yourself deep in the middle of an essay only to look over at the fluffy pen on your desk and stop working, you've fallen prey to human nature once more. Sadly, the Distraction Free Zone is a myth. Anything can and will be a distraction if your brain wants it to be, but this one hack saved my life . . .

SANCTITY OF SPACE

This is the idea that every space in your living environment has a purpose. When you lie in your bed, you're telling yourself to sleep. When you stand at the stovetop, you're expecting yourself to cook. When you're sitting at your desk, is your brain now expecting to do work or scroll on your phone?

Be disciplined in how you treat your space. If you want to quickly check your phone, physically stand up from your desk or move to the bed. Equally, if you're doing work in your bed, have a physical change which represents working, such as sitting perpendicular or moving it to a new location in your room.

The more you teach your brain that a certain place means work, the less distracted you'll be. I came to associate my desk only with typing, so I didn't crave scrolling in the same way I did when I was on the sofa watching TV. As hard as it may seem, the more disciplined you can be with yourself, the easier you'll make your life. Be strict to be kind.

If you don't have a desk or dedicated study space, that's okay! This mindset hack still applies. Last term at university, my bedroom didn't have a desk. To apply sanctity of space, I developed a ritual of physically changing my position in the room to indicate work. Rather than lying in bed or propping myself against the wall, I'd either sit on the floor on a yoga mat and lean against the bed or physically turn the bed to face the window. In either of these two positions, I would not allow myself to scroll on my phone. These positions were for work and work alone. When I took breaks, I would physically remove myself from the space or turn my bed around again.

If your home environment isn't optimal for work, develop Sanctity of Space in a location of your choice. I loved visiting my local library because it was my space to dedicate to schoolwork. I made a low-fi study playlist that I associated with my time there. Even now, hearing those songs puts me in the mindset to study! I was careful not to spend time in the library watching YouTube or scrolling through social media. Sanctity takes effort but eventually reduces friction.

Some schools offer homework clubs. A great way to develop a dedicated space to get your work done is to attend these. They often have the added benefit of accountability from peers, and you can ask for help when you need it!

Wherever you decide to study, help your brain physically associate that space with work. You'll be one step closer to making homework an easy habit!

HERMIONE-GRANGER-LEVEL ORGANISATION

What is the one thing which makes homework less painful that doesn't require you doing work? Being organised! Developing a system for where you keep your sheets or online files won't turn you into Hermione. It also won't mean you get your work done (sorry!). But it'll definitely make life easier.

Everyone has a system which works best for them – and no, unfortunately shoving loose sheets in a drawer is not classed as a 'system', even if it's what I did for years . . . If you prefer online files, you can develop a tree-like system of folders with clear titles. Start with the overall subject, such as 'AS level French', and then create a sub-folder within it for each chapter, such as 'Chapter 1'. Inside this, you can create further sub-folders if necessary, like 'Homework', 'Class Notes' and 'Flashcards'. You should be able to navigate through your subjects without stress.

If you are organising physical sheets, don't be shy: get yourself a ring-binder folder. During A levels, I ended up with at least two folders per subject. I used them so much that I gave them names, because calling a folder containing a pile of A4 sheets Frederick makes it slightly less intimidating. I developed a system where I would instantly file away sheets into the relevant folder so I was less likely to lose anything.

Tree File Organisation

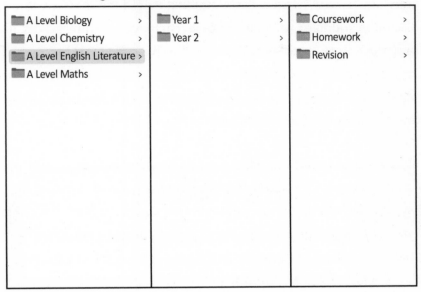

Friction is one of the reasons we procrastinate. Organisation leviosaaa-s it away.

MAKE IT FUN (?)

Here we put a tentative question mark. Go, have fun. Blast your music. Insert frequent breaks. Soak up the beauty of learning (sounds cheesy, but YES learning is amazing!). While the most effective, deep work isn't necessarily fun, it's okay to be less efficient sometimes and enjoy yourself. For more passive homework, such as making a poster or taking notes, you have all the freedom in the world to create an experience.

There's no getting away from the fact that homework is a necessary evil of life. Though I would have rather spent more time chatting with friends or chilling at home, I look back at my school days and know for certain that this habit-building taught me *so* much about discipline and hard work. From university work, to internships, to my career, learning to set the foundations back then was invaluable.

So, just like I made my forced bus journey every day a lively highlight, I'm sure you can make your forced homework a little less daunting. Or dare I say, fun?

PUT IT IN PRACTICE:

You've heard all about my strategies and hacks. Now it's time to quiz what you do and figure out what's working and what you might need to change.

Start by writing down what you currently do every time you want to get homework done.

- Do you have a specific place or time?
- Do you make a to-do list first, or complete work from memory?
- Are you using SAAD revision techniques when studying?
- How can you use SAAD techniques in the homework you have to do this week?

Now plan a new, realistic routine to road test. Choose a study space and commit to only using it for work. How can you reward yourself every day for completing your homework routine?

ADVICE FROM . . . PAIGE

Paige studied science and maths through to university, where she specialised in astrophysics at degree level. She is now working in the corporate world as an actuarial insurance consultant. When she's not designing actuarial spreadsheets, she likes to play clarinet and saxophone.

Nobody wants to be that person panicking when the teacher is collecting in an assignment they never knew existed, frantically thinking up an excuse better than 'the dog ate my homework'. Therefore my best advice for school homework is to remain organised and accept that it is often a bad idea to rely solely on your memory for assignment deadlines. With so many subjects and tasks to keep track of, it is easy to accidentally let one slip.

When I was at school, I used to religiously write down the details of all homework assignments in my school planner. I designed a standard format and jotted down the subject, teacher, task overview, date set and date due, with an asterisk alongside to draw extra attention to it in my planner. It only takes a couple of minutes to make a note at the end of a lesson and saves a headache later on as you scramble to remember exactly what work you need to do. It became a daily habit to review the planner so as to remind myself of outstanding assignments and tick off those that were complete.

This system allowed me to plan my homework schedule effectively, prioritising assignments due first and avoiding last minute panic when a deadline approached. I remember my classmates often approached me when they had forgotten details of homework, so I was clearly doing something right! In hindsight maybe it would have saved some hassle if I had got my friends hooked on this homework recording system too . . .

CHAPTER 8

HABIT
FORMATION

My first ever boyfriend cheated on me during the Year 12 mock exams.

Oh, I remember it too well. I was revising for an English literature exam. Little did I know that my own life was to become a Shakespearean tragedy. As night fell, slow and heavy like the world was being encased in lead, I turned on my phone. I was met with an onslaught of text messages from friends who had gone to a party the night before. The overuse of angry emojis in my notifications, mixed with a healthy dose of 'He's a d*ck' said it loud and clear: my boyfriend got with another girl at this party and didn't tell me.

There was no softening the blow. There was no waiting until after my exams. The truth winked at me on a screen and I was one tear-filled call away from being single.

Revising for exams is hard enough but the academic system seems to forget that we're messy teenagers trying to figure out our lives at the same time. The exam board clearly did not care that the English exam was not my only priority of the week.

That night, I stared at the ceiling until my eyes went fuzzy. I heard my teacher's voice in my head: 'Always get a good night's sleep before an exam.' But the last thing on my mind was revision.

I don't know if you've ever been through a breakup but my mind became an unhelpful showreel of the best memories of my relationship or, worse, an incessant voice nit-picking everything wrong with me that inspired him to cheat. Needless to say, every time I sat down to revise for the next few days, flashcards weren't exactly the first thing I thought of.

How then, do you balance schoolwork and life? How do you attempt to stay on top of work when you might be struggling with family problems? Or navigating toxic friendships?

The secret is setting up positive habits that look after your mental health. I'm not talking about taking a self-care bubble bath once a month to cure your depression (let's be honest, we love candles and face masks but they don't solve everything!). Instead, I'm talking about habits which implement mindfulness into your life. Habits that can help you monitor and manage your stress levels without the promise of quick fixes. They require discipline and open-mindedness. As we will discuss later in the book, mental health is complex and more severe conditions cannot simply be cured with mindfulness. However, mindful practices have been proven beneficial for many reasons such as fighting stress. Studies have shown that, if done consistently, meditation can help settle the anxiety you might feel walking into that exam hall or help you forget your friendship troubles for an hour or two by enhancing your ability to focus.

When I faced those relationship troubles during my exams, it was the practice of mindfulness that switched my mindset to one of heightened focus when I needed it. Checking in with myself became essential to process my messy emotions. It is tempting to wait until stressful moments to learn how to take care of your mind, but with a hundred things to do during exam season, I doubt you'll suddenly become a yoga guru. Let's learn how to form positive habits *now*.

WHAT IS A HABIT?

In this chapter, I'm going to explain what most people don't know: how habits are actually formed. If you've started a workout challenge but failed at day four (wow, I feel attacked), tried to set up daily revision and lasted a week (guilty) or attempted to turn yourself into a meditation guru to no avail (now this is just personal . . .), you will know that habits are not as easy to set up as choosing to do something and simply doing it. However, it is essential to understand the process of habit creation if you are ever to improve your day-to-day life.

Let's break down what a habit is . . .

. . . by starting with what it is **not**.

A habit is not just something you do every day.

Do you ever feel like you have to 'make yourself' do something? For example, you have a 'habit' of revising maths but always put it off throughout the day? That's how you know you don't have a habit – you have a responsibility, a nagging task.

Instead, habits are specific actions, often subconscious, that you find yourself doing in specific situations.

In *The Power of Habit*, Charles Duhigg describes how habits are formed of three parts: a cue, a routine and a reward. The cue is what triggers a certain habit. It's hearing your phone buzz and turning to look at it. That's a habit. It's going to the toilet triggering you to wash your hands (I hope . . .). It's how getting out of bed cues you to brush your teeth without thinking about it. The routine here is the action you then perform – in this case, brushing your teeth. It is practised, easy and requires no thought. The reward is the desired state you are trying to get to. It's what we crave before performing the habit. It's what leaves us feeling satisfied and it's why we're likely to do the habit again. For

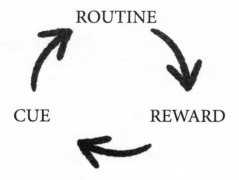

brushing your teeth, the reward is the feeling of cleanliness. The reward is what makes habits addictive – and we can use it to our advantage.

To illustrate the three parts of a habit and how crucial they are to making or breaking one, I want you to think about a bad habit in your life. Perhaps you wake up and instantly start scrolling on your phone, derailing any plans you had for that morning. Or, like me, perhaps your bad habit is that when you're doing work, you'll stop when it gets too hard and turn to social media instead, drowning your difficulties in the enjoyable distraction of the internet.

Welcome to a bad habit that killed me during exam season – and how I solved it.

I'd have a clear goal in mind: plan and write an essay. I'd lay out my revision materials. I'd diligently start planning. I'd read some notes. I'd even write the essay plan. But when it came to putting pen to paper and spending 90 minutes scribbling my heart out, I'd look over at my phone. I swear I heard it whispering. I'd find some excuse, anything that sounded productive, to turn my phone off airplane mode. I'd remember that I needed to text a friend back or that I recently posted an Instagram photo and wanted to see how it was doing. I convinced myself that I would look at my phone for only five seconds to do the task and then return, refreshed, to my essay.

Except that never happened.

Instead, I forgot about my 'productive task' the second my finger hit social media. Before I knew it, I was scrolling through the depths of holiday pictures and memes. Maybe throw the odd 'how to be productive' YouTube video in there just to numb my guilt. Time passed. My essay felt ever further away and the idea of turning off my phone and settling back into an academic mindset was too hard to fathom.

I described that bad habit as 'choosing distraction' rather than doing deep work. Let's break this down.

To understand a habit, you need to identify the components of the habit's loop. Only once you've diagnosed the loop can you look for ways to exchange old behaviours with new routines.

What is the bad habit? (Routine)

The first step is to identify the routine. In my phone-checking scenario, the routine is the most obvious part: it's what I want to change. My action, or 'routine', was to stop doing my work, switch on my phone and stay on social media, delaying or completely abandoning the initial task.

So that's what I put in the loop:

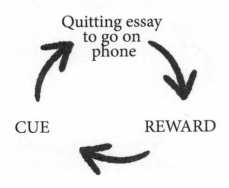

Quitting essay
to go on
phone

CUE   REWARD

Working out the cue and reward

But there are less obvious questions about this habit. What made me feel the urge to do this in the first place (cue) and what was I craving (reward)?

Was it that my essay question was so difficult that I didn't know how to start? Was I just bored? Was it always the same time of day? Had I already worked hard on other tasks and was fatigued? Was there a specific action on my phone that I was craving?

The only way to find this out was to experiment during my revision.

My first hypothesis for the reward I was craving was that I wanted to do something passive. In theory, if I craved a few minutes of not thinking then I could replace checking my phone with another task that gave me the same reward and return to writing the essay. So to test this, the next time I planned an essay and inevitably felt the need to pull out my phone, I'd challenge myself to try a new, replacement reward. Rather than going on social media, I would let myself abandon my essay and read a book.

If my theory about the desired reward was correct, then reading a fun YA novel could replace scrolling through social media, and

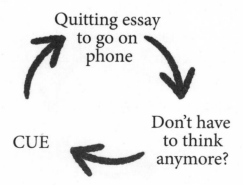

Quitting essay
to go on
phone

CUE

Don't have
to think
anymore?

this would have a less addictive quality. Hopefully I'd read for a bit and feel satisfied, ready to attack my essay with full force.

But it didn't work. Not only did I still crave my phone but I had zero desire to return to my work and, if anything, felt less motivated after taking a break from it.

So I tried again. The next time I came to write an essay, I tested the theory that my desired reward was social validation, which I got through reading comments on social media. Rather than going on my phone, I left my desk to find my brother and chatted to him for 20 minutes.

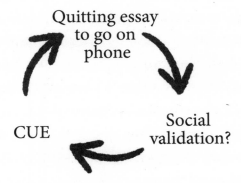

This was enjoyable and another easy break from academic work. But alas, my motivation for essay-writing was gone too. Even after socialising, all I wanted to do was go on my phone.

But then a new thought occurred to me. My revision schedule was always shaped in a way that meant I wrote essays in the mid-afternoon. After a whole morning of flashcards and past papers, I was dragging my tired brain into a taxing thought process. It was no surprise that, after a day of thinking, all I wanted to do was passively scroll on my phone. So perhaps I needed to look at my cue: I was tired and craving a reward of switching off.

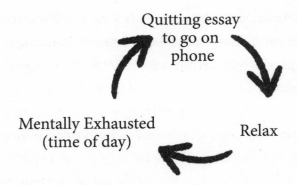

Quitting essay
to go on
phone

Relax

Mentally Exhausted
(time of day)

The next day, the essay was the first task on my to-do list. I breezed through the essay plan and was amazed that the familiar feeling of mental fatigue that had previously stopped me writing wasn't there anymore. Rather than finishing the essay plan and reaching for my phone, I felt motivated to fill the blank page with my ideas. I powered through the essay without a break and felt mental clarity in the process. As soon as I finished it, I scheduled an allocated period of 30 minutes where I could then check my phone and scroll through social media. The reward? Enjoying the luxuries of the internet without any guilt.

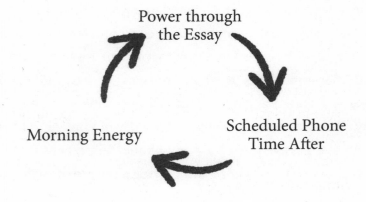

Power through
the Essay

Scheduled Phone
Time After

Morning Energy

This process was incredibly clarifying. On the surface, the cue seemed to be the difficulty of the work or the enjoyment I got from my phone. In reality, it was *when* I was writing the essay that was the issue.

From then onwards, I only ever scheduled essay practice in my mornings and made sure to give myself a passive break afterwards. I came to crave the satisfaction of finishing an essay, knowing I had scheduled time straight afterwards to do well-earned nothing.

I always scheduled a full hour to do nothing during my mid-afternoon slump of the day as I realised no activity was productive then. Rather than allowing guilt to impact my other activities, scheduling chilled time made my day happier.

So here, we break down the process into four steps:

1. Identify the **routine**. What is the bad habit you want to change?
2. What is the **cue**? This cue is almost always a location, time, emotional state, the people around you or the immediately preceding action. Examine your own habit and the context in which it happens and you'll be one step closer to figuring out why you do it.
3. What is the exact **reward** you are seeking? What kind of feeling does the current reward give you? What might work in its place that will be better than what you are doing at the moment? Experiment until you've found something that sticks.
4. Tackle the bad habit with a rigid **plan** – and stick to it. It was up to me to schedule my essay-writing into the mornings from then on, rather than falling back into the habit of shoving them into the time when I would be having a mid-afternoon slump and inevitably crave my phone.

James Clear, in his book *Atomic Habits*, goes further to say:

Make your cue obvious.

Make the endpoint attractive (craving).

Make the routine easy.

Make the final reward satisfying.

Obviously certain habits are more difficult to change than others. However, having a deeper understanding of what makes up each habit allows you to attack them with meaning. The best way to create a good habit is to shift an existing one.

HOW TO MAKE NEW HABITS STICK

Just like it's important to identify the cue of a bad behaviour, when you attempt to set up a new, positive behaviour it must be preceded by a consistent cue to make it stick. For example, it's unlikely to be enough just to say you will meditate every day. Each day looks different and so one day you might do a meditation upon waking up but the next you're fumbling around at lunchtime to do it. The 'habit' will not last longer than a few days. This is why New Year's resolutions often fail – because there's no consistent plan for implementation. No wonder I never wrote this book four years ago . . .

The best way to have a consistent cue is to **attach the desired habit onto an existing habit,** one which may be subconscious. For example, I always make my bed when I get up in the morning. It is a habit. It makes my room look cleaner, and I do it without thinking.

But what about revising the definition of standard enthalpy change of formation? I can definitely say that was not part of my daily routine!

Instead of labouring over when to review that definition, I made it a habit to repeat the definition in my head while making my bed. Every. Single. Day.

Of course, the first day or two, I was fumbling over words and had to check my flashcard in between folding my sheets. But after a few weeks, it was so ingrained I could have said it in my sleep. It has been two years since I reviewed that definition and to this day, I can still repeat it in my head. **Make it a habit. Give it a cue.**

Some more ideas for cues are reviewing posters or flashcards every time you have breakfast. Odds are, you're eating something every morning so you already have an existing habit that you can tack a new one onto. So, rather than going on your phone, make it part of your routine to go over some questions you set yourself. The chilled environment makes it less of a chore and an easy refresher to get your brain started in the morning.

You could decide to read your English literature book every day on the bus to school. You might do four maths problems as soon as you get home. Whatever it is, attach it to part of your daily routine. That's the only way it'll stick.

SUGGESTIONS FOR POSITIVE HABITS

So now that you have a better understanding of how habits are formed and why you need to tack them onto existing habits, what are the positive habits that saved me during exam years at school?

I preach a lot about mindfulness, not because I'm a hippie who thinks our only purpose in life is to be happy (okay, maybe a little?), but because mindfulness is proven to be grounding. The thing is, most people only want to implement habits like meditation when they hit a time of stress or anxiety. Why should I meditate every day of the school year when I'll only be stressed during exam season?

You see, habits are formed through repetition over time. Imagine you're in that week of exam season where you have 12 exams. You're stressed, desperately cramming and not looking after yourself as well as usual, the last thing you want to do is learn how to meditate. Way too much effort. Nope. You need to set up good habits *now* that will be tried and tested when you need them.

So back to meditation. Bear with me.

While it has its roots in ancient India, Taoist China and Eastern practices, modern-day meditation is not reserved only for spiritual practice. I can feel many of you rolling your eyes at the idea of 'wasting your time' by just sitting and breathing. It sounds uncomfortable. It sounds useless. Surely we all breathe all the time anyway? Why would you need to focus on it?

The answer is simply: because there is nothing more grounding than your breath.

I can still feel the eye rolls.

Think about how many distractions you face on a daily basis. You're checking your phone or thinking about tomorrow. Your thoughts are often occupied without you even realising it. Meditation invites you to be wholly present and to observe whatever feelings are there without judgement. It's not about forcing yourself to be happy (did someone say toxic positivity?). Instead, it's about being mindful of whatever you're experiencing. The reason this is powerful is because we often suppress how we feel. In the age of social media trolling, highlight reels online and cultural norms which lead us to put on a brave face, we do not always acknowledge our feelings. In times of stress, this is detrimental and leads us to bottle them up.

You don't have to express your feelings to anyone if you don't want to but meditation is a way to truly notice where you're at and make peace with it. It invites you to refocus and recentre your mind in a healthy way to remind yourself what is important.

As a perfectionist who struggles with anxious thoughts, meditation has changed my life.

So how do you meditate?

You don't need a fancy app to be present but I do recommend guided meditations and breathing techniques until you begin to master the process. There are many free guided meditations on YouTube, and apps such as:

- The Honest Guys – a YouTube channel with some of the best free guided meditations for learning to be mindful.
- Yoga with Adriene – a YouTube channel with amazing beginners' yoga and meditations.
- Headspace – this app has a free and paid option with accessible meditations for beginners around various topics, such as dealing with stress.
- Calm – great meditation app, especially to help you fall asleep.
- Insight Timer – a free meditation app with contributions from practitioners all around the world.

Turning off all distractions, you get comfortable in a seated or lying down position and close your eyes. You focus on breathing in and out through your nose, slowly inviting yourself to deepen the breath. Breathing techniques like inhaling for six counts and exhaling for eight counts can be helpful to focus your thoughts on the present moment. You don't judge your thoughts or strictly try to change them; you just notice them. You remind yourself that they are just thoughts. They don't have power over you. There is strength in accepting how you feel.

I love the idea of seeing your thoughts as clouds passing through the sky of your mind. Thoughts are impermanent. You can observe them from afar and notice their shapes, but you can also let them go.

If meditation is a habit you wish to implement, I recommend making it the start or the end of your day. Dedicating five-to-ten minutes immediately upon waking up or just before you go to sleep allows you to reflect and set intentions. It is a practice which has been proven to increase your attention span (revision will thank you!) and contributes towards a happier life.

You don't realise it, but you are training your attention span every day. Every time you go on social media and swipe before something finishes, you are teaching yourself that it's okay to lose focus when something gets boring. This is natural, of course, but if you don't train your brain the *other* way, it becomes incredibly hard to focus on long-form academic work. Meditation is an excellent brain-training exercise.

Here is a breathing technique called 'Square Breathing'. Breathe in to the count of four, hold for the count of four, and then breathe out of for the count of four. You can set a timer for five minutes and repeat this. Ta-da! You're meditating.

For a similar reason, I love yoga to pair the mental aspect of meditation with moving my body in a meaningful way, especially

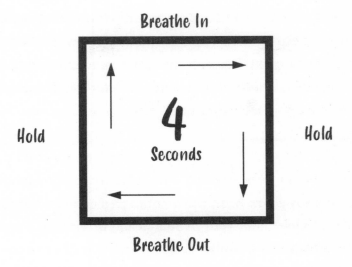

when I've been sitting in an uncomfortable plastic school chair all day. For example, you can turn square breathing into simple yoga by raising your arms to the sky when you inhale, stretching upward when you hold your breath, and letting your arms fall again on the exhale. Repeating this simple movement will connect your breath and body to make you feel calmer.

CHOOSING YOUR NEW HABITS

So there you have it. You're now a professional Habiteer. I'm sending you a mental sticker of congratulations. *"Great participation."*

In all seriousness, you can understand this process and still suck, horribly, at changing anything long-term in your own life. If you stop your positive habit for a day or two, do not fret. This is normal and recoverable. If you stop for a week or more, re-evaluate the cue and look to change it.

But most of all, get honest with yourself in reflecting on how you spend your time. If you can dedicate a few hours a day to passive scrolling (my screen time says I definitely can . . .), why can't you find five minutes – just *five minutes* – each day to set up a routine for your mental health?

PUT IT IN PRACTICE:

1. Identify a new habit you want to implement – whether it's to look after your mental health or develop a more robust study routine.
2. Break down the habit into its loop. What will you choose to cue the habit? Will it be a specific time and location? Will you chain the habit onto an existing habit in your daily life?
3. What reward will you crave when you do this new habit? It can be as simple as the satisfying feeling of finishing what you need to, knowing you can freely relax afterwards.
4. Get practising the habit. Learning how to implement habits *now* will be so helpful for you in exam season and beyond!
5. And finally, if you can't get it to stick straightaway then don't panic. You haven't 'failed' because you miss a few days. If you really can't make it part of your routine perhaps you need to try a different cue – move the time or location you do it or tack it onto a different existing habit. Experiment, like I did when I wanted to stop looking at my phone instead of writing essays!

ADVICE FROM . . . VARAIDZO (VEE) KATIVHU

After completing her undergraduate degree at University of Oxford, Vee is studying a Master's in education at Harvard University. She is passionate about student learning, access to education and encouraging others in minority positions to take up space. With many demands, good habits are key to her success.

When forming habits it is really important to understand that you must first create the right systems. It will be difficult for you to build a new habit if the systems around you are weak. To build a system you need to identify the problem you want to solve first. For example, you may have an issue with organisation and keeping on top of your study environment and as a result you are finding yourself spending each day tidying your desk, your room and your sheets of notes. Instead of waking up every day and tidying your room and desk (rather time-consuming tasks) you should try and find a system which avoids your room becoming messy altogether. For example, having folders for your notes that are divided according to the modules you are learning in school, and are colour coordinated so you know where each subject of notes lives. Or getting a desk drawer divider so that your pens can live in one section, your notebooks in another and your electronics in the other. This way, whenever you are finished using your notepads, you can put them straight back where they live. You are now forming the habit of putting the items where they belong, in your newly functional organising system. This system now helps you to feel less worried about spending hours tidying your room before starting your studies. Instead, you now have more time to focus on what really matters: the work. That's the important thing with habit building, you must have a reason for what you are doing whether you want to make your life easier by adopting new and healthier habits, like going to sleep on time, spending less time on your phone or implementing more exercise into your routine.

I motivated myself to be consistent with good habits during secondary school by knowing what my end goals were. I wanted to be happier, healthier and more in control of what was happening around me. The more sleep I got, the happier I felt, the more time I spent outside walking or running, the more energy I felt I had. Building healthy habits became a crucial part of my life in order to achieve my ultimate goal which was to make my life easier and the tasks I had to do more enjoyable. Having to study for exams was no longer difficult as I had already made my revision notes throughout the year, rather than scrambling at the last minute. So wherever possible, focus on finding your problem area first, the part of your life you would like to improve and become happier in, figure out what system you can put in place to achieve that, then begin slowly putting it in place and watch the magic happen!

Good luck!

CHAPTER 9

PERFECTIONISM AND FEAR OF FAILURE

Year 10. All eyes fixed on the sheets of paper in her hands, the teacher zigzagged through the room, matching test papers to names. I didn't see students' faces fall as they took back their marked test. I didn't hear students squeal with delight at the green-encircled grade at the top of their sheet. No. I watched the teacher, waiting.

The second she placed the test paper on my desk, I snatched it away from prying eyes, eager to deal with the result alone first. My face fell. All those hours of revision for nothing.

'What did you get, Jade?'

'How hard did you find that paper, Jade?'

I mustered a smile and a breezy laugh. *Act cool. Just tell them.*

'Oh my gosh, I got higher than Jade!'

'Wait, how did you get *that* question wrong?'

'Weren't you predicted an A?'

To the pleasure of onlooking students, I had not done as well as I wanted to.

I shrugged back into my chair, not wishing to make eye contact with anyone, and silently cursed myself for not revising harder.

The last thing I wanted to do was go through the paper with a fine-toothed comb, focus on my mistakes and learn from them. To me then, mistakes were not an indication of where to grow.

They were a direct attack on the image I had of myself as a good, reliable student. My dreams of top grades seemed further and further away with each mark of red pen.

Perhaps perfectionism began here. Or perhaps it began as early as Year 7 on that fateful day of the academic year when report cards were received. Slipped into each of our planners was a roadmap of our academic standing, complete with every grade we achieved, our future predicted grades and a barrage of comments to try harder. Report cards were a direct indication of how you were doing – and how well teachers thought you could do.

Soon that report card would be in the hands of my parents. They'd bring last term's report card out of nowhere and silently compare. My dad never finished secondary school and he always emphasised how much he wished he'd been given more opportunities to get an education. He was brought up in a farming community where, in his father's eyes, the real work began when he got home from school each day. My dad raised me to know that university was a privilege he didn't have and so desperately wanted me to have. And though my mum never put real pressure on me, perhaps it was the way her eyes scanned the report cards, counting the number of A*s or As, that made me add her hopeful gaze to the pressure I put on myself.

I wanted to make my parents proud. We all do.

Between peer reputation, teachers you don't want to let down, and parents' expectations that we desperately wish to meet, we develop a fear of failure.

We all know the feeling of opening a test paper and not understanding anything. We're all familiar with the jolt of anxiety, the way our heart rate picks up or the way we suddenly start telling ourselves about failure. We know what it's like to say, 'I won't be able to get that grade,' or, 'Why do I even bother revising?'

For so long, I attached my worth to my grades. I thought they were a direct representation of my intellect and work ethic. In reality, grades are just an opportunity to see where you're at. They're the most useful indicator of what you do and don't understand, allowing you to guide your learning and do better next time. From that point of view, failing more is good. It's not about the grade you get along the way but rather how you react to and learn from it moving forwards.

Failure is a tool for growth, nothing more.

When I was studying abroad in Berlin last term, I saw the same sticker plastered on lampposts across the city: '**Learning is productive failure.**'

That's all failure is. A chance to learn.

But when failure is attached to career prospects, your opportunities and the expectations placed on you by loved ones, it's no wonder we can't see failure in any positive light.

Fear of failure manifests itself in a reluctance to try new things, get involved in challenging projects or properly commit to your goals because you're so scared they won't be actualised. It takes courage to pursue big goals and even more to declare them publicly. It's like laying yourself on the line, knowing you could easily fall short.

'I'm aiming for a 9, Mrs Warner.'

'A 9? Wow, well I can't wait to check in with you on results day!'

Fear of failure shows itself in other ways. You might start to self-sabotage, to procrastinate. The more we commit to and put into our work, the higher the stakes. We push away tasks and delay deadlines to the future version of us because we are scared to start in case it all goes wrong.

One of the biggest symptoms of fear of failure is perfectionism, which is something I struggled with for most of my school career and still do. There is too much friction in starting something if you know you want it to be perfect. Perfectionism is where you labour over the small details rather than prioritising the big picture. It means you'd rather restart something because this version is just not good enough, or you don't ask for help because you're reluctant to show anyone a version which isn't final.

In my life, perfectionism cripples me. It is the reason I often make a YouTube video, fully plan, film and edit it, only to decide in the crucial last few seconds that it's not good enough to be watched. It's the reason I spend a few extra hours on revision even after I probably know the concept well enough. But most of all, it is the reason why grades which were certainly good just weren't good enough to me. If a grade was worse than the one I got before or didn't match whatever standard I'd imposed on myself, I couldn't bring myself to be happy. Because perfection doesn't exist. Perfect is self-defined. You are reaching for the top rung of a ladder which is constantly getting higher because here's the thing, you can always be *more* perfect.

'Perfect is the enemy of good,' said Voltaire.

And I couldn't agree more.

GOLD-MEDAL PERFECTIONISM

Before we butcher the idea of striving for perfection, it's useful to acknowledge why it's useful. Even if it stems from fear of failure, at its core perfectionism means caring about your work – a lot. Caring means trying hard. It means being attentive to where you went wrong and always wanting to do better. It is often the reason why we put in an extra hour of work. In a new study of nearly 10,000 students aged 12–21 years old, they found that perfectionism predicted better academic achievement. Perfectionists have a better work rate and are more likely to set ambitious goals. We love goals.

However, perfection comes at a price. Where one goal stops, another starts. What begins as a healthy challenge ends in unhappiness because you can always challenge yourself *more*. Achieving 80 per cent is amazing but the lure of 85 per cent is stronger. Perfection feels like you're climbing a set of stairs to a defined goal destination. You're lifting your heavy legs every step closer. The goal is in sight and so you keep walking, even when you're exhausted. Rather than taking breaks on the staircase or stopping to admire the view, your eyes are fixed on the destination. You keep trudging along.

But when you finally get there, a new set of stairs appears out of nowhere, enticing you higher. Rather than patting yourself on the back for reaching your goal, you feel a new stress associated with the next goal destination. Once again, you do not take in the present view. You level your eyes to the new destination, even more tired than before, and begin walking to the next goal.

And it's exhausting. The focus shifts from the journey to the endpoint. You don't stop to take in the wonderful parts of the process because you're fixated on winning. And finally, when you eventually achieve what you want, the pride you feel is limited. Your brain is formulating the next goal. There is always more you can do.

Ambition is plagued with a fear of never achieving 'enough'.

Aaron Beck was the creator of the famous cognitive behavioural therapy (CBT) model which is one of the most influential frameworks in modern-day therapy. He developed the basic cognitive model with four interplaying facets. When I discovered this, I realised that the methods I used to channel perfectionism into something useful was in line with this framework. Although it oversimplifies things a lot, it is useful to start to understand how perfectionism manifests – and tackle it.

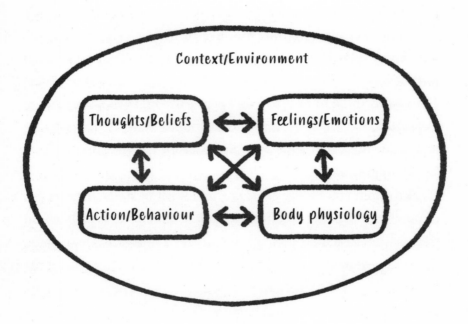

Many people believe that their thoughts are caused by their feelings and emotions but, as this model shows, what we are experiencing physically also affects our thoughts. Feelings do manifest in our body physiology – for example, increasing our heart rate – but this in turn impacts the emotion we label ourselves as feeling. The double-headed arrows indicate that each of these elements is 'bi-directional', meaning they all influence each other. They create something called 'reinforcing feed-back loops' which means as one increases, the other increases and so on. They keep increasing each other unless an external factor intervenes.

How you uniquely experience perfectionism or a fear of failure can be mapped onto the diagram. For example, let's examine self-sabotage after receiving a bad test score. Due to an aversion to failure and unhappiness at receiving a certain grade, you are scared of the next exam. You don't want to receive another grade you are unhappy with. You carry with you the belief that: 'I will not do well in this next exam.' This thought causes you to feel anxious (feeling), which causes your heart rate to pick up (body physiology) and you can't focus anymore. In your panicked state, it is much easier to choose not to revise (action) due to stress. You cannot think rationally, nor plan useful revision. This only makes you feel more anxious, which makes focusing even harder. After not revising, you likely do worse in the next exam (action). This confirms your belief that, 'I will not do well in the exam,' which demotivates you further, meaning you try even less next time.

To break this model of self-sabotage, we need to tackle one of the cognitive elements. For example, you can replace the initial limiting belief with a strong thought of, 'I am capable of achieving X grade. I am worthy of being successful.' To cement this thought, you can repeat it to yourself like a positive affirmation multiple times a day. This thought will lead you to feel more confident (feeling), which increases your ability to focus (body physiology),

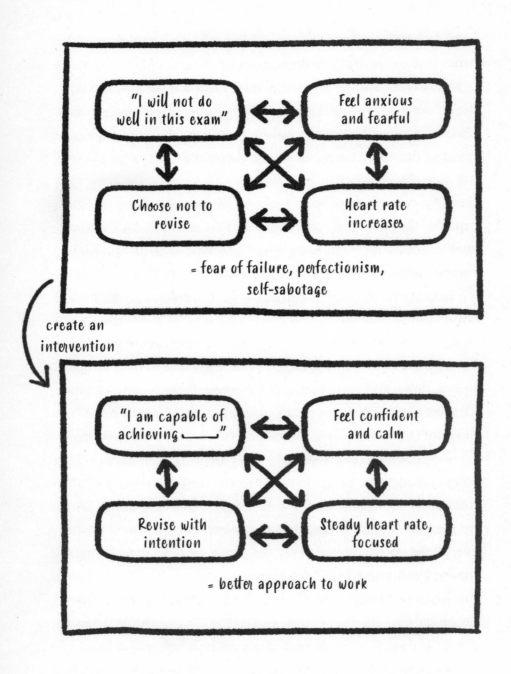

helps you revise with intention (action) and thus reinforces your belief that you are competent (thought).

Equally, you can tackle a different element of the framework if you do not have control of your thoughts. Start with action. Using the methods described in chapters 3 and 4, create a robust revision timetable and practise SAAD revision techniques. Stop overthinking the possibility of failure. Instead, study with intention and create a new belief that you are working hard and are capable (thought). This makes you feel more confident (feeling), enables you to focus more easily (body physiology) and continue revising with intention (action).

Perfectionism goes hand-in-hand with validation. One of the reasons we try so hard to improve by micro-grades is not because achieving one more mark will get us into a better university but because we've come to define our self-worth in achievement. If you describe yourself as a B-student, you're attaching your identity to the letter on a piece of paper. It's no wonder you're desperate to collect marks at all costs: your identity depends on it.

This relates to the twin mindset framework I mentioned in chapter 1. Approaching your abilities as static relates to a fixed mindset. You believe that what you are capable of is pre-defined by genetics or luck. Mistakes reveal your natural capability, so every time you fail it is a reflection of your incompetence, rather than something to learn from.

So the first trick to move beyond perfectionism is to develop a healthy approach to failure with a growth mindset. Can you remember the key word associated with a growth mindset from chapter 1?

It's *yet*.

I don't understand this *yet*.

I haven't got the grade I want *yet*.

But I will. Getting things wrong is how I will get there.

The growth mindset is a belief that your abilities can be developed. It is an important shift to *improving* your abilities rather than *proving yourself*. Getting better grades is amazing and we should all strive to challenge ourselves. Adopting a growth mindset is a healthy way to go from seeing your worth in your grades to seeing failures as a springboard for future learning. And, as you focus on learning from your mistakes in a productive way, grades will come as a natural by-product.

If you must be a perfectionist, learn to be an *adaptive* perfectionist, as described by three psychologists Mobley, Slaney and Rice in a paper on the merits of perfectionism (2005). The mark of a successful adaptive perfectionist is that they view their abilities as constantly growing and changing the more they learn. Set goals, have high standards for yourself, but don't define yourself in them. Be preoccupied with **growth**, not failure.

HOW TO COMBAT PERFECTIONISM

Firstly, acknowledge that you experience it. If exams and the expectations around them scare you, or if you're not using your time as effectively as possible because you want to do everything *right*, then that's okay and it's important to admit that to yourself.

The Pareto Principle – 80/20 Rule

It's funny how in all the phases of your revision, 80 per cent of your knowledge comes from 20 per cent of the total time you spend. Think of all the time spent producing notes, flashcards, or trying to understand content. Sure, it's all necessary. But only the most active, most SAAD moments of revision, are contributing to actual marks in an exam. When presented with a difficult question, it won't matter how beautiful your notes were, only how much you retained for this moment. Productivity is recognising which study activities contribute the most to getting marks in an exam and optimising for them.

The 80/20 rule suggests that **80 per cent of the product (grades) comes from 20 per cent of the input (revision).**

As a perfectionist, it is tempting to do every revision technique you can think of to maximise your grades. The more scared you are to fail, the more time you will likely spend on studying the same concepts over and over.

But much of that revision is unnecessary. The Pareto Principle invites you to identify the *most* meaningful elements of revision and prioritise them. Do them when you have the most mental capacity. Work them into your regular routine using spaced repetition. These activities will help you get to 80 per cent of the understanding.

In his book *The 80/20 Principle*, Richard Koch explains that 80 per cent of our happiness is experienced during 20 per cent of life. We don't receive substantial joy from every hourly activity in our 24/7 existence, like cleaning the bathroom or sleeping. However, small moments in that day, the 20 per cent, are what generate enough happiness to make it a good day. When we go to sleep that night, we can focus on those little moments which made us feel good, thus optimising for the activities which give us emotional benefit.

Imagine you were writing a book (hi, hello), 80 per cent of the benefit received by a reader comes from 20 per cent of the process – writing the first draft. Sure, an author can spend 80 per cent of their time labouring over every word choice, refining details and overthinking design choices, but this will only add around 20 per cent to the reader's experience. The bulk of the reading experience is derived from the basic, but important, foundation of getting words on paper. From this point of view, optimising for efficiency would be to make more time for writing and less time for overthinking each word used. Get the message down and get 80 per cent of the benefit in. Get to the perfectionistic 20 per cent later.

There is so much content to learn for every subject that memorising 100 per cent of all of it is no easy task. Knowing all the major themes and characters of the English literature set text is straightforward but pulling apart every meaningful quotation and studying every scene requires much more time and effort. Generally, 80 per cent of the content is straightforward to revise using the most optimal revision techniques. But getting that final 20 per cent as well? This is where perfectionism creeps in.

It's about not just knowing the concept but knowing the *exact wording the mark scheme wants*.

It's not just understanding all mathematical concepts in class but knowing *how to apply them in a novel question*.

This takes strategic thinking and more work. But to get to this point, you need to get confident in the first 80 per cent of your knowledge first.

So how do we use the 80/20 principle to approach revision?

Imagine you're revising for an end of chapter test tomorrow. What type of questions will be there? Are they weighted differently, such as a 2-mark and an 8-mark style question? Where are 80 per cent of the marks coming from? Is there an essay component worth more? Is there a type of maths question which garners more marks, such as the topic of integration or differentiation?

Analysing mark production is a way to game the system like a top student.

If you prioritise your initial energy into where you'll get 80 per cent of the benefit, you will perform phenomenally better while juggling other subjects. For example, if, in your English literature revision, you can learn how to deeply analyse five literary techniques and be able to apply at least one of them to almost any text or question, this will serve you better than memorising 30 techniques you cannot confidently apply. Start small and prioritise. If you're aiming to smash the pass grade, focus your energy not on every tiny detail of the syllabus but rather exam technique and understanding big concepts. What 20 per cent of your revision will get you 80 per cent of the way to that pass?

When structuring your revision time, the trick is to **identify what the most efficient output-producing activities are and optimise for them.** If you know that the revision technique blurting greatly improves your knowledge of scientific concepts, plan to do more blurting! If you know highlighting text takes up a lot of time but does not produce worthy results, decrease how often you do this.

To engage in 80/20 thinking and beat perfectionism, we have to keep asking ourselves: what is the 20 per cent that leads to the 80 per cent? We can then use 80/20 thinking to change behaviour and to focus our attention on the 20 per cent that counts.

Perfectionism is rooted in wanting to get 100 per cent all the time, which is okay. In fact, this is awesome to aim for. But the 80/20 principle is a reminder that getting to 80 per cent is amazing, and it's about optimising. The last 20 per cent is detail-orientated labour.

If you are aiming for top grades (9s and A*s), you will need to care about details, the small marks lost and the nit-picky, time-consuming elements of the content – this is the less optimisable 20 per cent which requires a fine-toothed comb. But applying the 80/20 principle to the revision techniques which will get you there is a great start. It says, let me stop worrying about the perfect outcome and just systematically work towards *most* of my knowledge first.

Consistency and resilience

Not every day is going to be the best revision day of your life. And yet, when you have clear goals, you may want your revision to feel 'perfect'. So you do all the right things – including making a detailed timetable, planning your revision in advance and sticking to set times.

But what happens if something throws you off track? Say you've planned a revision activity from 3pm to 3:15pm and your previous planned study goes over. It's tempting to abandon the whole thing. When you've planned the rest of the day or you feel overwhelmed by the amount that needs to get done, you can feel a notion of failure in not meeting your own little deadlines.

So this was not a 'perfect' revision session. But you showed up. And that's more important.

2:30pm – 2:55pm	Blurt German vocab
3:00pm – 3:15pm	Type up history notes
3:15pm – 4:00pm	*went wildly over and abandoned next task*

Once again, perfect is the enemy of good.

It is far more powerful to revise frequently than for every study session to go as perfectly as planned. You can learn to be agile, readjust your timetable and keep powering through. If you find a task more challenging than expected, note that down and keep trying.

Do you remember the idea of spaced repetition? Our memory decays over time, so the more we revisit information at slowly increasing intervals, the more likely it is to enter our long-term memory. To beat perfectionism and optimise the science of memory, aim for consistent revision. Five average days of two-hour revision are better than one 'perfect' ten-hour session every two weeks. As was mentioned in chapter 8 when we talked about habit formation, the more resiliently you can show up and do the work, no matter how imperfect it feels, the more successful you will be.

You won't always get 100%, no matter how much revision you do. Not every test result will feel like one you're proud of, and that's okay. Failure teaches you far more than success and for every disappointing percentage, there is an invitation to learn resilience, to remember that you are more than your grades, and to fall in love with the process. When life throws you challenges beyond your school years, you'll be able to recognise that imperfection is where growth occurs. And we like growth.

Trying to beat perfectionism can be a lifelong journey, but you can take effective steps to help overcome it. Firstly, you need to **define what 'enough' i**s and make your standards of 'good' focused not on the final outcome but the **process**. If you are working hard, optimising for SAAD revision techniques and taking care of yourself, *that's* perfection.

Special shoutout to the student reading this who just 'failed' a test, had a mini breakdown from not understanding something or who wants to soften their goals because they believe it is not for them. You are doing incredibly. You are not a failure. Treat this mini setback not as a reflection of your incompetence but as feedback to learn and try again. Realise that you're not there yet, but you can be. Review which activities in your life are most likely to contribute to your success. Map out the cognitive model affecting how you work. And then keep trying.

PUT IT IN PRACTICE:

- After reading this chapter, do you identify any perfectionistic tendencies in yourself?
- How do you normally react to failure?
- Write out the cognitive model for what you're thinking, feeling and doing when you normally get something wrong. How would you ideally like to react in order to embrace this failure in a positive way? Write it in a new diagram.
- What is the most productive 20% of the work you do which contributes to 80% of your learning? How can you optimise for these activities? What are you sacrificing to achieve the last 20%, and is it worth it?
- Do you ever abandon your revision because you didn't perfectly stick to your plan? How can you learn from these mini failures productively to stay consistent?

ADVICE FROM . . . RUBY GRANGER

Ruby was one of the pioneers of the online community StudyTube. She is studying English literature at Exeter University and is passionate about mental health and making studying fun!

Perfectionism can be a good thing. A really good thing – especially in hustle culture. But, as with so many aspects of hustle culture, it can also be damaging – and I've definitely struggled with that darker side to perfectionism. The side that isn't mentioned in job interviews. You've probably been over-told that 'perfect doesn't exist' (my teachers told me this every parents' evening!) and yet still we pursue it relentlessly, striving after something which maybe isn't even there. 'Perfect' for me has always been something super abstract. It's never really been attainable. When I got 99 in a test, I'd want 100; when I got 100 UMS, I'd want 100 per cent; even when I got 100 per cent, I would beat myself up about some sentence which didn't make sense or a case study I'd forgotten to include. We have a tendency to deflect what is 'perfect', meaning we never quite reach it and end up dissatisfied time and time again.

The thing I've struggled with most as a long-term perfectionist is this notion that I could have done better. At school especially, I was forever telling myself that I would have done better if only I'd done a few more hours work or read that extra paper or prepared that little bit harder. And yes, you might score higher if you do these things – but there's a huge difference between how hard you CAN work and how hard you should WANT to work. Back in Year 10, when I was preparing for my first history topic test, I spent my half term poring over my books, learning every last bit of information. I cancelled plans, studied through a family holiday and worked so late that I made myself ill. I learned the material as 'perfectly' as I physically could and I got 100 per cent for my efforts – but at what cost? Looking back, I wish I hadn't got 100 per cent because of what I sacrificed to get it. Before starting a project, I now ask myself one crucial question: how much do you want this? How much time am I willing to sacrifice? What things are more and less important than this? Being mindful of these priorities is so important and can help you to stop a task before toxic perfectionism comes into play. It's my number one tip as a long-term perfectionist.

CHAPTER 10

MENTAL HEALTH

Every day in the UK is kept exciting by our provincial mystery: the weather. Waking up and flinging open the curtains is a lucky draw. Is that a peek of sun, I see? Oops – just kidding! Another wash of grey.

No matter what the weather looks like, we get on with our days. Sometimes we fall into step with the rays of sun and the day is transformed. Sometimes it's more challenging – cue Year 7s running from one school building to another in pouring rain, balancing PE bags and food tech bags on tiny arms.

We know that every day, the weather will be slightly different. We get the odd good day, followed by the odd bad day. Sometimes we get long periods of one type of day which we call 'seasons' or 'spells'. But we always know the weather is there, a part of daily life, and what it chooses to bring us each day is not permanent.

I don't know about you, but I never went to bed wondering, 'What will my mental health look like tomorrow?' like I might do with the weather forecast. There was no internal check-in. My brain was always just . . . there. It didn't even occur to me that it could change. But as the onset of winter brings gloomier days, so too can exam season bring a spell of stress – and with it, a new pressure on your mind.

Mental health, like the weather, is always there. Sometimes good, sometimes bad. Sometimes easy, sometimes hard. While we can't control the environment that produces weather patterns, we can control how we react to the conditions that turn up, from slathering on sun cream to packing an umbrella. So too can we control how we react to our ever-changing minds. Every time you ask, 'What's the weather like today?' can you also ask, 'How do I feel today? Where is my mind today?' Just like looking out of the window at today's weather, observation of your mental state is the first step to reacting accordingly.

But there is a fundamental difference. We Brits talk about the weather almost every day but mental health is never the topic of small talk. We don't pop to the corner shop and ask the cashier where their mind is that day. We don't even ask our friends. The weather is a shared, universally recognised experience but we've convinced ourselves that mental health is ours and ours alone to deal with. It is a language only we can learn, expressed not in text or tongues. Becoming fluent feels like a scary, lonely, solo endeavour.

WHAT IS MENTAL HEALTH?

Mental health affects how you feel, think and act (vague, right?). Simply put, mental health means how well your mind is functioning overall. And it's precarious. It's affected by everything from stress to how much sleep you get, to the amount of blue light you receive through going on your phone.

One of the reasons we overlook mental health is because it is a lot easier to look after what you can see. If you have a cold, you take a day off school. If you break your arm, you don't feel embarrassed to ask for help. But mental health? With intangibility comes stigma, and stigma means staying silent.

There is no tick box or formula for achieving good mental health. In fact, good mental health is not a fixed thing that you can 'achieve' and tick off your list. Instead, your mind fluctuates daily, like the weather, and that's normal. Our mental state is often a reflection of how we react to daily life, such as how we handle stress and interact with others.

Feeling overwhelmed every now and then is absolutely normal. It might mean that you're taking on too much or that you care a lot about what you're working on. However, feeling persistently low starts to shape your overall mental wellbeing. Diagnosable mental health disorders like anxiety, depression and OCD change your day-to-day perception of life and are connected to hormonal imbalances in your brain. Experiencing these issues does not define you but can make daily life a lot harder.

This chapter recognises that each of us is incredible and capable, and yet presented with unique mental challenges. This individuality is not appreciated by the standardised exam system, which does not always accommodate our barriers.

Welcome to this safe space chapter! I will touch on my own struggles with mental health, how that intersected with academic stress, how I handled it and how I wish I'd handled it. This feels like I'm laying myself out on a lab tray to dissect my personality and the things that shaped me. I'm terrified. I have written and rewritten this over and over, uncertain what I should share. Some of the stories in this chapter have never been voiced, not in the online confines of my YouTube channel or with friends.

I hope this chapter helps someone out there struggling with mental health, be it their own or that of a loved one.

If there's one thing I want you to know coming out of this chapter, it is that you are never alone. If you're feeling overwhelmed, you're not alone. If you wake up each day with no motivation, you're not alone. If you wake up each day thinking more deeply about your weight or physical appearance than exam grades, you're not alone. If you compulsively overthink the number of minutes you spend revising, you're not alone. You are valid. You are never to blame for struggling with your mental health at any point in your life. Clinically diagnosed mental health issues can be a by-product of hormonal challenges or deficits in neurotransmitters in your brain, and it's important to recognise that mental health isn't solvable by 'choosing to be positive'. Nice try, motivational quotes.

But I didn't always think this way. There was a time when I didn't think mental health existed. There was a time when I thought struggling made you weak and that acting strong fixed everything. Before I dig into my own mental health at school, I am going to share a story which shaped how I viewed mental health. It is vulnerable, and it is not just my story to share. I am grateful that my beautiful mum encouraged me to include this experience, a story which is hers just as much as it is mine, because she believes that it could help any of you who are going through similar things with those you love.

When I was 13 years old, my mum started drinking. I didn't know much about alcohol, so I thought finishing a bottle of wine a day was normal, a stress reliever, even. The slosh of maroon in a glass became the familiar backdrop of the evening. After a while, I realised that alcohol was not my mum's friend. It did not want the best for her, or us. What began as a quiet respite and a chorus of 'cheers' at the dinner table gained a life of its own. You see, wine was slowly stealing my mum.

I remember coming home from school to find her sitting on the floor, bottle in hand, sobbing. The first few times, she'd hastily swipe away tears, force a watery smile and ask about my day. Other times, it didn't go like that. I never knew what to do. My dad worked late. I did not want my younger brother to see her like that. Everyone in my life knew my mum as positive and cheerful, which she really was most of the time, so I learned to hide bottles. But I also hid what was happening.

If she spoke of ending her life, I laughed like she was joking. When she whispered that we'd be better off without her, I'd say she was being silly. Those years are a blur because rather than acknowledging her comments, I would do my best to forget them. Anything that tarnished my view of my mum was not allowed space in my brain.

One day, Mum started to tell me that she was depressed, which at the time, I equated to 'feeling sad'. It felt like a slap in the face. By my selfish logic, if you feel sad, you do things to make you happy. I couldn't understand why she couldn't just *choose* to be positive. Did she not see how hard this was for me and my brother?

Fourteen-year-old me did not know what depression was.

Fourteen-year-old me did not understand mental health.

The only thing that angsty fourteen-year-old me promised to do was never to burden anyone with my mind and always choose happiness if it was there. I became the 'Positive Hardworking One', so positive that my cheeriness could sometimes penetrate the cloud hanging over the bottle; so hardworking that a good grade could lighten the mood. When I had friendship troubles, faced bullying at school, questioned my appearance or my body, I tightened my hairband and got on with it. When I didn't understand something at school, I'd work overtime until I did, all for a good report card – I wanted to make her happier.

Through no fault of my own, I did what was perhaps the worst thing for all of us. Rather than listening to my mum, validating her mental health and seeking help, I chose to pretend it was not real. Smiling cheery smiles was just easier.

When one of your parents needs you to be strong and positive, you don't make them feel like you need help. So for me and the people I loved, I remained Positive Hardworking Jade. Any thought patterns which strayed from that image were mine, and mine alone, to deal with.

I am so proud to say that my mum has been totally alcohol-free for years now. This incredible woman taught me so much about what it means to navigate the trials of your mind and how to be both vulnerable and strong. She always gave us the utmost love and selflessness even when things were tough for her.

But the way that I think this translated to my life is that I really, really, really suck at reaching out for help, even still. I'm excellent at independent things. Anything that relies on routine is mine. I will happily meditate daily. I will get myself to sleep on time and I will check in with where I'm at. But what I'm still learning to do is realise when my own brain might be too much for me. I am chronically independent, proudly so. And that's the issue. I hold myself in such high regard that I am convinced I can cope alone. I can cook the family dinner *and* study hard *and* look after people in my life *and* keep myself sane. Oh, and stay positive, *of course*. The thought of burdening another with my mind is terrifying.

This mindset led me to put undue pressure on myself to succeed. In refusing to recognise my mum's mental health, I also refused to recognise my own.

The first step to coping with mental health – both yours and others' – is to acknowledge its existence. Only then can you seek help and develop habits that will be useful for you. When my mum told me she was depressed, I should not have laughed. I should have supported her to seek professional help. When I felt like academic pressure was becoming too much, I should not have seen expressing that to others as placing a burden on them.

As humans, we're not too rational. We always do what we think is best but *best* is influenced by our fears. We're scared of appearing weak or incapable, of alienating those we love and of admitting to ourselves that we're not okay. We think we're fine because fine is relative. Sure, we're still breathing. And yes, we can muster a smile when necessary. If we're not on death's door, or even if we are, it's easier to keep trudging along than to address the voices in our head.

One in four students in England will experience a mental health issue of some kind every year. One in four. Struggling is actually statistically normal.

All four out of four people have mental health. Your mind today will not be the exact same mind tomorrow. Check in. Check in with yourself and the people you love and listen with an open mind. I'm so proud to say that my mum is doing much better now. My parents are the most supportive, beautiful people in the world and I'm so grateful for everything they've done for me. Everyone struggles with their mental health at times. The rough patches do not define who we are.

The mental health challenges we face beyond the academic system can be challenging enough but when they intersect with the expectations of exams, what was a manageable state of mind can cascade into something vicious.

When I was doing my GCSEs, there were times when exam stress felt suffocating – like each exam was a boulder on my chest, crushing out my breath. I became scared of my own brain.

In the lead up to exams, I started having *the dream.*

You know the one, where you're in the exam hall, you open the first page and you can't answer a single question? Everyone around you is writing frantically and the sound of pen on paper is the only thing you can hear. You feel your heart racing in your chest, swelling like it will explode, forcing your eyes to stare at the paper in front of you until the words blur.

As my GCSE exams approached, I nearly cried every time I didn't understand a concept in my notes. It's harder to be patient with yourself when you feel like time is running out. I have vivid memories of holding flashcards in my hands, shaking. My bedroom was both a space to relax and, increasingly, a space to stress. The line got blurrier over time. The door was shut. The desk was covered in papers. The Post-it notes on the window hid the sun. I felt surrounded.

I never spoke to anyone about how stressed I was. To my family, I was fine. As I explained above, I was always 'fine'.

The group chats would ping and I would reply with emojis. I didn't have it in me to reply with words and, as time went on, I stopped reaching out.

In the lead up to the start of exams, I was militant, ticking off tasks and timetabled study sessions with practised ease. I went to see my English literature teacher a week before my English exam. I entered her office, practice essay in hand, with a mission. I needed to understand a specific theme in the text and there is nothing more helpful than a teacher going through your work. The staff room was empty aside from her and a pile of textbooks. She put down her lunch, took my practice essay and got out a red pen. I sat beside her, fidgeting as she scribbled notes in the margins of my essay. My leg started its classic nervous-tic, filling the staff room with the sound of it bobbing up and down.

When she looked up from the paper, I was not expecting what came next.

'How are you, Jade?'

'Good,' I said instantly, forcing a smile. 'Exams are a lot, but I'm fine.'

She kept looking at me. 'Are you sure?'

I nodded. I couldn't maintain eye contact. I felt like she could see through my smile.

She looked a little longer and then nodded too. 'Okay.'

She returned to marking the paper. I tried to focus on her pen flicking across the page. She started reeling off advice, areas where my essay was weaker and how I could improve. Even though I was listening, I couldn't stop thinking about her question. It made me feel so insecure. For the first time, I could hear myself truly questioning, was I okay? Sure, I was studying according to my trusty timetable. And yes, I would cover all the content before the exam. And of course, I had been paying attention all year. So why didn't I feel more confident?

'Jade?'

Her eyes were back and I realised I had zoned out. 'Mrs Dobbs, I'm terrified.'

The second these words left my mouth, heat rose through my body. I felt the tears coming. I tried to look anywhere else. I tried to swallow them. I tried coughing and fiddling and thinking about happy things but before I knew it, I was sobbing.

The teacher put down my essay and let me cry.

I spent the whole lunchtime telling her what I was going through. I felt so invalid being scared about exams, especially when there were much bigger things going on in the world. I kept talking and she continued to listen.

There was something so cathartic in letting everything out. I expressed the thoughts that were keeping me up at night, the pressure I felt from peers and family and how anxious the thought of exams made me. My teacher reminded me that she couldn't sit the exams for me. She also couldn't change how much they meant for later life. But what she could and did do was listen. It was like a weight was lifted from my shoulders. After I expressed my feelings once, it suddenly made talking about them much easier.

I remember taking my snot-covered essay to the girls' toilets before my next lesson and staring at my red face in the mirror. I looked tragic but felt relieved. I wiped my puffy face, straightened my uniform and went to the lesson with my head held high.

There is no worse feeling than being the odd one out at school. Whether it's a plaster on your face, feeling insecure about a new pimple or, in my case, having obviously been crying. It takes a level of confidence to ignore other students. That day, I didn't care. When friends asked if I was okay, I was honest. 'I'm really scared about exams.'

'Oh.' The girl next to me said. She paused. 'I actually went home and cried every day this week.'

'Really?'

'Yeah. I'm so scared.'

The more I started to open up to others about my feelings, the more I realised that everyone felt the same way. Friends who I thought hardly cared about revision were secretly struggling to sleep. One of my best friends had sought out a therapist without me even knowing. Teachers spoke of stress so generally that it felt like no one was *actually* affected by it in the way I was, but the more I invited open conversation, the more I realised that was untrue.

Exams are stressful.

I don't know who you are, what your situation is or what challenges you've already faced beyond having to take important tests. But what I do know is that you're not alone. Right at this very second, there are many students feeling exactly how you are, hiding their fears behind headphones and smiles. There are students who feel like their feelings aren't valid. There are students terrified they won't live up to the expectations of those they know and love – or simply meet their own.

If there is one thing I have learned in all my time studying, it's that you can't isolate yourself emotionally. We all want to think we're invincible and that we know ourselves better than anyone. 'Why burden others with our feelings? Why show ourselves as weak?' we think. We idolise people who seem to have it together. We think people who don't care about school are cool. Secretly, everyone has it together less than you think.

If you're reading this and you're feeling stressed, firstly know that you are incredible.

The academic system tricks you into thinking your worth is defined by a grade or an exam performance. This is a lie. Like Einstein said, you cannot judge everyone by a standardised system. You have an entire personality and array of interests and talents that won't be captured in these exams. Maybe you're the comedian in the family, able to brighten anyone's day with a joke. Do you know how amazing that is? You have talent that exams will never capture. Maybe you're an incredibly kind friend. Sure, the exam boards don't take this into account, but every relation-ship in your future life will remind you how valuable that skill you possess is. Start to see yourself in the broader context of life beyond this system.

Secondly, everything will be okay.

It sounds so annoying, I know. You often hear, 'Exams aren't the be-all and end-all,' or, 'Life is so much more than exams.' Clichéd, overused and so unrelatable in the moment that these platitudes have no real meaning.

You can agree with these statements but it doesn't change the fact that exams *do* matter and they *do* determine the stepping stones of your future life. This is undeniably true. But it is impor-tant to remember that everything will still be okay. Whether you get glowing grades or no grades. Whether you get full marks or miss a grade by 1 per cent. I truly believe that everything in life works out exactly as it should. You will find your path in whatever next step you choose. The people you meet, the things you'll learn and the experiences you have will all follow from these moments. And you likely won't regret them.

If you're in a narrow bubble of thinking, challenge yourself to see more broadly. Do your revision but don't attach yourself too greatly to the outcome. Focus on the learning and growth this period of your life is teaching you.

As Shakespeare wrote in *Hamlet*: 'There is nothing either good or bad, but thinking makes it so.'

Exams are just pieces of paper we give meaning to. Your brain is too clever and twists everything further than it needs to. Whatever that piece of paper holds, the world will not end. You will succeed, you will be loved and you will have a future. A good one. Expressing how you feel to other people is an amazing way to have your thoughts rationalised.

OPENING UP? NO, THANK YOU

It's all very well hearing that we should talk to people about our mental health struggles, big or small, but in practice, it's a lot harder. One question that went through my mind often was: at what point is this bad enough to make it worth asking for help? When I felt anxious or unmotivated, it always felt within the realm where I could deal with it alone, so I never reached out.

Looking back, that was a problem. There's still a stigma around mental health, so we feel pressure to justify it as being 'bad enough' to warrant conversation, as though we need to prove our struggles are real. In reality, there is no level of stress you need to reach for your feelings to be valid enough to discuss.

Speaking to others halves the problem you have been magnifying in your own head. For example, I used to tell myself that I wasn't working hard enough. I would feel guilty whenever I did things with friends that didn't involve work, flicking my eyes to the clock every hour or so as though the falling seconds were currency I was wasting. However, I never expressed that guilt. I would half enjoy my hangouts with friends while secretly growing anxious about the piles of revision waiting at home.

One day, I decided to tell my friend how I felt. Though it seems like a tiny thing, sharing my thought process was like opening the folds of my brain and inviting someone inside to judge its colours. Her reaction made me doubt why I'd ever questioned sharing my worries. She reminded me that I needed to take breaks in order to be truly productive – something I knew but had forgotten. From then on, there was a mutual understanding between us. It made every subsequent meetup more meaningful and I felt supported.

Talking about your mental health struggles can also make other people who are going through similar things feel less alone. You sharing your feelings is sometimes enough for someone else to feel validated in theirs. There are so many reasons why people struggle to open up – be it different cultural expectations, the influence of toxic masculinity or the need to be seen as strong. Many languages do not have a word for mental health. There is often no word to describe depression or anxiety. Without a label, it's easier to convince yourself that your struggles aren't real. Without a label, mental health continually fails to be recognised. If your parents think that mental health isn't real or that struggles are just something that have to be 'pushed through', then

I'm sending you a virtual hug. Because that's tough. When you're struggling, the last thing you want is to have to convince others your feelings are real. I want to remind you that your mental health is valid, however it feels. Use the power of the internet to reach out to mental health charities, find a local counsellor or speak to a trusted professional at your school.

If I could go back and speak to 16-year-old me, I'd look her in the eyes and tell her that she doesn't need to struggle through exam stress alone. I'd tell her that just because she has felt the need to support others in her life, it does not mean her own struggles have to be faced alone.

Whether it's diagnosed mental health issues or sustained periods of not feeling like your best self, it's okay not to be okay. It really is. You're still you. But, remember that you don't have to go through it alone.

ADVICE FROM . . . EHIS ILOZOBHIE

Ehis is a final-year modern languages student at King's College London. Seriously, the number of languages this guy speaks is incredible! He makes hilarious, ingenious videos about uni life, fashion, comedy and social commentary. Here, he was vulnerable enough to share some of his own mental health journey.

If I could say one thing to Ehis between ages 14 to 18 it would be: You Matter.

More than grades, more than extracurriculars, more than accomplishments, more than applications and more than rejections.

The cyclical nature of academia that we all are conditioned into is something that is so easy to become invested in, to the extent where we see mental health and our emotional wellbeing as 'after thoughts'. In the middle of term or revision during exams, accompanied with stress, worry, anxiety, doubt and overthinking, as much as we plan ahead, someway and somehow we end up in the same position. Forgetting that our best is all we can give and putting everything ahead of our health is simply damaging.

It's really bitter sweet that it was only at university I really understood how important it is to intentionally create space for my mental wellbeing and make it a priority of mine, but

I'm glad that I did because I have never been better than I am right now; this doesn't mean that the low days go away but it means that when they come I know what to do to pick myself back up and take one step forward, even if it's just one step I have the capacity of taking that day.

I have categorised this into three steps: The Talk, The Rest and The BAM! (trust me, you'll get it once you get it) and I hope this helps anyone reading this.

The Talk:

As much as we're all main characters in our story, it is crucial to know that in that story we're not alone. There are so many forms of support around you that it's imperative you make use of all of it.

When I'm feeling incredibly stressed I drop what I'm doing and pick up the phone almost immediately and talk to my parents. Now being a second-generation migrant means that the conditions both of them are used to in relation to academia means they don't necessarily understand exactly what I'm going through but they listen – and sometimes in the midst of feeling overwhelmed, it feels really good for someone (outside of the pressures of studying) to just listen. Also, no one else can reassure me of my abilities and remind me that my best is all I can simply give like my mother and in times when I'm crying on the phone doubting myself, those conversations of reassurance can really lift my spirit.

Next to family and friends, I've come to learn that another great support system can be the school/college/sixth form/

university. I deal with both anxiety and mild-to-extreme depression, which started around secondary school. This meant that I would sometimes get incredibly overwhelmed in class when I didn't understand something and would rather have the ground open up and swallow me than to raise my hand and ask questions. I'm slowly coming to learn (still learning, even in my final year of a four-year undergraduate degree) that no one actually cares in those moments and I'm just the one stuck in my own world but upon coming to university I made sure I made the most of lecturers and seminar tutors. If I don't understand something and I don't have the courage to ask a question in front of the seminar, I'll simply stay behind after the class to ask my question and if they don't have the time at that moment, they ask me to see them at a more convenient time.

The hardest thing for me was accepting that I needed more support outside of family, friends and teachers. Counselling and therapy are not accessible to everyone and I completely understand that. But if your institution offers it, I can only advise you to make the most of it and try it out. The first steps are incredibly difficult. (After my first session I actually cried and didn't go back for two weeks but hey! We've grown!). To deal with the stresses of growing up, whilst making decisions you think will impact you for the rest of your life (some actually will, others really won't) is very scary and having someone to guide you through the mess that is your emotions and help you understand what you're feeling and how to navigate that can be really beneficial to you and your emotional wellbeing.

Rest:

I really hope my Father doesn't read this because I don't want to hear I told you so. I can't let him have this one.

Growing up, I used to pride myself in being the King of Multitasking. Read at breakfast, homework during lunch and revision whilst having dinner. Throughout all this my Dad was always quoting this line that I genuinely thought just existed to piss me off: 'Rest is productive'.

Now it's something I repeat to myself and my friends when we're overworking ourselves. Your body and mind can only take so much and if you push it past the point of capability it can cause long-term damage. We're all athletes somehow and resting is crucial.

Get in those hours of sleep rather than trying to function on four hours of sleep. Instead of trying to get through those flashcards on the bus, put on some music and just take in the scenery. It is so important to have multiple pockets of rest during the day where you shut down and literally allow your mind and soul to just breathe. No work, no stress, no worry but just vibes. Trust me – you'll thank yourself later.

Finding Your BAM!:

Anytime I talk about this everyone looks at me weird but just give me a chance and I promise it will make sense.

I think of the BAM as a driving factor outside of what I do. I would say a hobby but in this day and age it's so easy for those to become stressful. Your BAM can be one or many things.

This can range from knitting or photography to reading for leisure, and so much more.

You want to find something you genuinely enjoy – for me its video editing and cooking – that you can almost use to push yourself through the tough times. During exam season I push myself through hours of revision and reward myself with two hours of just editing, one of my friends does it by baking something every weekend and another friend's BAM is dancing.

It is important that you make this something that:

You enjoy

You find relaxing

You leave feeling better

Helps you forget about everything that worried you

So that's the idea of the BAM. Use this to think what can your BAM be? Also don't think that your BAM can't change! I had a period where it was gardening but I quickly realised that's not for me and I wasn't good at it either so it was stressing me out.

These are just three things I wish I knew and implemented throughout my journey as a student. It's a very rocky journey and sometimes it feels like everything is crashing around you and you're alone but trying to do these three things at least once every week has become an integral part of my life and has honestly helped me so much in being mindful of how I'm feeling, and I hope and pray it does the same for you!

CHAPTER 11

THE NIGHT BEFORE AN EXAM

Wow, you made it!

All that revision, all that hard work. And you're here.

We all know exam season hits like a truck. It's something about the expectations it carries or the build up over the years which makes it feel like the be-all and end-all.

The night before an exam is less about the revision you do and more about how you set yourself up. You need to think of yourself as a warrior going into battle. It's no longer enough to have good techniques or extensive training, you now need to be well-rested, healthy and mentally prepared to tackle the challenges ahead.

This is why the night before an exam is a fine balance between last minute revision, and not allowing yourself to get stressed.

We all know Y2K self-care: put on a face mask and slip into a bubble bath or grab your mates and play video games for hours, and suddenly the internet proclaims you less stressed. While self-care for you might involve skincare, that face mask can act as a real mask. Nowadays we love quick-fix self-care instead of getting to the root of how we're feeling. Are you eating well? Drinking enough water? Getting enough sleep?

Exams are hard. You want the most optimal version of you in that exam hall. Start seeing your body as a tool, a weapon, a key to unlocking the best parts of your brain. Imagine that guzzling water is fuelling your memory recall, eating fruit and vegetables is increasing your mental clarity and that every hour of sleep is a ticket to another question right. In reality, it's not always easy to stay healthy during exam season but treating yourself as your priority will definitely make a difference.

Are you an all-night crammer? Everyone has their ways, but when you've got a 9am exam, mate, just get some sleep. Sleep is good. Actually, it's bloody incredible. Feeling like you're not going to collapse from exhaustion is heavily underrated. We have a natural bias towards seeing more time spent revising as more effective once we get into the exam hall and discount the power of sleep or rest. However, sleep is the time where information is processed and memories are solidified. Without a period of inactivity in your brain, anything you tried to learn will decay more quickly. In his book, *Why We Sleep*, Matthew Walker explains how important it is to view sleep as productive. Rest has important long-term health benefits, yes, but it will also give you the optimum brain for that exam hall.

STRATEGIC LAST-MINUTE REVISION

Can you remember the three phases of studying for exams from chapter 4?

I dare you, test yourself, we can wait . . . ;)

Did you get it?

First you need to **understand** content. Then you can memorise or **learn** it. And lastly you **apply** it to exam-style questions.

Ideally, the night before an exam is no longer about understanding. Nope. You want to optimise time by using active recall SAAD revision techniques like blurting and flashcards. Most of all, start applying. Get your brain in the right zone by completing past paper questions, making sure to analyse any last-minute areas of confusion. I recommend timing yourself and pretending it's the real thing, especially because doing questions in a more comfortable environment beforehand makes exams feel less scary.

Before every exam, I would go through all the past papers I had done, specifically looking at the MARCKS analysis (see chapter 4) and the notes I had left myself on what to revise further. This would remind me of common questions I often got wrong or frequent weaknesses of my essays.

In my final revision, I would write a list of mark scheme answers word-for-word that I constantly got wrong. These were answers to common exam questions or concepts which needed refreshing. I called it my cheat sheet, even though I never took it into the exam hall! It was my golden sheet of paper. My lifeline. On the morning of the exam and on my commute, I could casually read through this sheet of gold dust and prepare my mind for success.

For peace of mind, consider making yourself a last-minute cheat sheet with all the niggling points you want to go over in the final moments. The process of making it is useful to pick out what you really don't know and rereading it on the day gives you peace of mind.

Although, if you're going to call it a 'cheat sheet' out loud, maybe be careful who's around – you don't want to start rumours . . . !

Here is an example of a cheat sheet I made for a chemistry exam:

Remember...

○ Bronsted – lowry <u>acid</u> = H^+ <u>doner</u>

Bronsted – lowry <u>base</u> = H^+ <u>acceptor</u>

○ $pH = -\log [H^+]$ Strength and concentration
of acid are <u>NOT</u> the same thing!
strength = how likely to <u>FUlly</u>
                   <u>DISSOCIATE!</u>

Higher Ka = <u>STRONGER</u> acid   (lower = weak)

Higher Ka = eqm   further to the <u>right</u>   (favours forward
                                      reaction)

○ $Kw = [H^+][OH^-]$
$\quad = 1 \times 10^{-14} \; mol^2 \, dm^{-6}$

Buffer = solutions that can RESIST small changes in pH.

e.g. alkaline buffer = weak base + <u>SALT</u> of that base

○ e.g. NH_3 w/ammonium salt ($NH_4 NO_3$)

                                  <u>You've got this gal!</u>

CHECK, DOUBLE-CHECK AND TRIPLE-CHECK

The night before an exam, we are in the business of stress reduction. Any element of the exam process which produces fear is an area to tackle. Is there anything more stressful than forgetting your calculator on the day of the science exam or waking up late thinking your exam is in the afternoon when it's really in the morning?

I am historically unprepared and far too spontaneous for my own good but the one thing I forced myself to do before every exam was to look back over my exam timetable and double check *when* my exam was and *where*. I learned this the hard way. When I was doing my Year 10 mocks, I was running late for an exam and convinced myself it was in the main hall. My previous exam was there, so it made sense the next one would be there too. I went through the whole process of putting my bag in my locker, collecting my exam resources together and steadying my nerves as I found the queueing point outside the door. The clock ticked by. None of my friends turned up. I was so wrapped up in repeating the points on my revision checklist that I didn't notice the teachers failed to appear. There was no register being taken. No usual bubbling fear. It hit me like a slap in the face that something was wrong, and it wasn't my friends, the teachers or the exam boards. It was me.

I finally got out my exam timetable, terrified I'd gotten the wrong time. My eyes scanned the page and landed on what I needed to see: 'sports hall'. I blinked, just to make sure I was reading it right. There it was, loud and clear. SPORTS HALL. As in, the building at the complete opposite end of the school.

I've never run so fast in my life. Any onlooking Year 7 would have thought I was training for the Olympics. I arrived at the hall in a puffing mess and saw my last classmates enter the building. Though I was met with scolding, I was quickly registered and plopped into my seat just in time to go through the rules of the exam. My heart was still recovering from its half-marathon and I could hardly focus on the questions in front of me, but at least I made it.

If I had been five minutes later, they wouldn't have let me in. I had the realisation that this could have been a grade sacrificed not through lack of revision nor laziness but carelessness on the day. All those hours of revision would mean nothing if I wasn't even allowed to *try* the paper.

Call it overkill, but from that day on, I checked my exam time-table at least three times before an exam.

Plan your wake-up alarm accordingly, know how you're getting to the exam hall and identify all the resources you might need and make sure to pack your bag. Exams are stressful enough as it is. So be that boring over-cautious person who checks, double-checks and *triple*-checks the logistics. Catastrophe? Averted.

Here's an easy checklist to help you to prepare:

- [ ] Pen (black)
- [ ] Pencil
- [ ] Clear pencil case
- [ ] Ruler
- [ ] Rubber
- [ ] Maths equipment (e.g. compass, protractor)
- [ ] Calculator (if necessary)

- [ ] Water bottle (with label removed)
- [ ] An analogue watch (optional, but recommended)
- [ ] Check the time of my exam
- [ ] Plan when I will wake up and how I will get there
- [ ] Check where my exam is
- [ ] Double check
- [ ] Triple check

STRUGGLING TO SLEEP?

Earlier I mentioned sleep. Sounds easy. Except the simple reminder to 'get enough sleep' can feel frustrating if falling asleep is near-impossible for you right now. I vividly remember the feeling of lying in bed before an exam, an ache in my chest and a heaviness in the pit of my stomach which was entirely unique to tests. Multiple times, I had nightmares about exams. Everything from the classic failing results day dream to my phone going off in the exam hall – even though I knew I wouldn't bring it into the room. When an event is so grossly anticipated by teachers, peers, parents and yourself, it's natural to be terrified. It means you care. But if you're struggling to sleep, here's what helped me and my friends.

Firstly, **get off your phone**. Stop checking live updates on Twitter. Stop playing into the panic on the group chat. It's fun to feel part of one big terrified collective but sometimes others' fear inspires your own hysteria. Be kind to yourself and stay away from the bubble.

Secondly, have a proper **bedtime wind-down**. If you've been revising all day, put away your work, play some music and attempt to take your mind off it. One of my favourite things to do was blare music through my headphones and dance around my room in an embarrassing, but happier, mess. We all need a release during exam season and exercise of any kind will clear your head.

Thirdly, find a way to **express** how you're feeling. The worst thing you can do is keep the fear bottled up, swimming around in your head with nowhere to go. I love creative writing and journaling; it helps me process life. I had a little notebook (a very aesthetic, gorgeous notebook, might I add) which I'd religiously throw my emotions into each day. Everything from feeling like I'd failed the exam, to a comment my friend made that I couldn't stop thinking about, or being so certain that the teacher would be disappointed in me. However irrational my thoughts, I let them flow into that notebook.

When I finally finished, I'd look at everything I wrote and almost chuckle. Sometimes you only realise how irrational your worries are when you put them on paper.

I would always finish a journal entry by writing what I was grateful for. It could be big or small. It could be the fact my mum made me dinner when I was stressed or that I had a clean, soft bed to crawl into that night. I would be grateful for the summer light, illuminating my past-paper-filled room.

When you orient yourself into a space of gratitude, you cannot feel fear in the same way. The more deeply you write about what you're grateful for, the more you'll start to feel it. And in appreciating your life, even these tough moments, you'll have the strength to face the exam tomorrow. After all, how lucky are you to have an education? We get the chance to not only learn but demonstrate our knowledge in a way that's meaningful. Without all the unnecessary stress and hype, that's pretty cool. Not everyone in the world gets to learn.

Other ways to express your feelings include art, playing an instrument or even making YouTube videos like I did during exam season. Give yourself an outlet that's not just scrolling through social media. In processing your feelings, you'll find it easier to fall asleep.

Again, I know I'm making it sound easy and sometimes it's not, but I promise this three-step process will make you feel better. Get off your phone, have a bedtime wind-down and find a way to express your feelings. Exam season is not a sprint but a (long and evil) marathon.

THE MINDSET FOR SUCCESS

One of the most underused mindfulness techniques is positive visualisation. It's that cheesy thing that is easy to dismiss as having no tangible value. But here's the tea: it works. There's so much literature providing evidence for the power of mindset and all the most successful students I know use this tool to set themselves up for success. There is a branch of human memory called Hebbian learning. It's pretty complex stuff, but the basic idea is that the more you think of something, the easier it is to think the same thing again. We have lots of nerve cells in our brains which are responsible for creating and transmitting thoughts, and the more we use the same nerve cells, the more they start to work together. When you repeatedly use a certain pattern of thought, you are making it more accessible. For example, if you think about what you're grateful for every single day, you are making this thought process easier to access. On the flip side, when you stop using certain nerve cells together to produce certain thoughts, you are less likely to think these subconscious thought processes again. If

I stop telling myself I'm stupid, I'm making this thought pattern less accessible. Use it or lose it. Welcome to neuroplasticity.

The reason this is powerful is because it lets you break old ways of thinking about exams and take conscious control over your approach. It allows you to make your brain a friend, a trusty accomplice, rather than an enemy.

Your brain is so powerful, far more than we currently know. Various academic literature in the space of neuroscience shows that self-affirmation has a high correlation with performance. If you repeatedly ask students to write about their closest values an hour before an exam, they will perform better. If students wrote about why values like love, knowledge and kindness are important to them, it would positively affect their academic performance when regularly repeated over time. The underlying confidence you have in yourself preceding a scary event can and will affect how you do – so how do you optimise this?

A book which was useful to me in secondary school was Dr Joe Dispenza's book *Breaking the Habit of Being Yourself*. Though this book has elements I am sceptical of, his discussion of how your thoughts and feelings interact with your current behaviours was a useful framework to question my mindset towards learning.

Dispenza discusses how every time you have a thought, there is a biochemical reaction in the brain that releases specific chemicals that cause you to feel a certain way. For example, thinking about exams brings back memories of the fear you felt when you last took a test. You vividly remember the feeling of not being able to answer a question and, without you realising, your body reproduces this feeling of fear. Thinking about how hard tomorrow's exam will be causes you to feel scared. As we begin to feel the way that we are thinking, we think more about how we're feeling. We reinforce the feeling of fear by approaching the exam with more thoughts of fearfulness. If exams always make you feel stressed, your brain refires the exact same neural patterns that they were wired to in the past. You begin to relive past feelings of stress and you train your body to remember the emotional state you were in the last time you encountered an exam. Your past is now becoming your future and your emotional reaction turns into a habit without you even realising.

If how we feel and react to exams are an unconscious auto-pilot based on past experiences, the only way to get out of that unhelpful narrative is to unlearn your old thinking patterns and rewire the brain to new, better thoughts. We have to *think greater than we feel.*

When you think about doing well in an exam but feel in your heart that it won't happen, you're only halfway to the mindset you need. Ideally, you need to work towards aligning your thoughts and feelings. The night before an exam, focus on directing your thoughts to a place of success. And then to go beyond just thinking: use all your imagination to *feel* what it would be like to succeed in this exam. *Feel* how proud you are. *Feel* how calmly you approach each question. *Feel* what it is like to keep working at a question methodically even if you don't know the answer. Your emotional engagement with the upcoming exam will help prepare your mindset for success and reduce your likelihood of blanking.

Every night before an exam, I would lie down and do a positive visualisation meditation. You can find these for free on YouTube or use a meditation app. You can also just play calm music and focus on the upcoming exam. You want to imagine yourself in the exam but as the most successful and calm version of you. Imagine yourself slowly turning the pages, taking your time to read the questions and looking at each one with a deep feeling of: *I've got this.*

Imagine yourself finding a question that you don't understand and instead of panicking, calmly working through it using whatever knowledge you do have. Imagine yourself being logical, trusting that somewhere in your brain you have the jigsaw pieces to get somewhere on this question. Imagine writing an essay with the affirmation, 'I have an abundance of time. I am not pushed for time.' Though you can still write quickly and work with efficiency, setting your brain up to believe you have all the time that you personally will need is a way to make yourself feel more relaxed.

Imagine yourself finishing the paper and daring to smile – not because you got every question right but because you genuinely know you did your best. Imagine leaving the exam hall and feeling *proud.* The more strongly you can visualise the event in a positive way, the more likely you are to embody this visualisation when it comes to it.

Without realising it, you're already visualising the exam right now, just probably in a negative way. Work to replace your existing feelings towards the exam hall with more positive ones and watch your attitude to exams shift.

We have been conditioned to need a certain grade or result to make us feel like we are a good student. We feel like we need a tangible reason to be proud of ourselves. However, that is allowing the external world complete control over how we feel internally. Instead, we can start by feeling proud of ourselves now, no matter the result, and suddenly our approach to exams changes. The fear of the result has no power over us. We feel grateful for trying and we stop attaching our self-worth to the end result.

Why do you need to wait to achieve 100 per cent to know you worked hard? Can you start feeling proud *now* and treat that final grade as a bonus?

A TEST OF CHARACTER

Our modern exam system has become not merely a test of content or knowledge but also a test of character. They test your discipline and work ethic, but most of all, your ability to look after your mental health. Exams challenge you to deal with stress and try to be the best version of you, even when it seems hard.

Exams don't need to be as stressful as we all make them out to be. You can choose not to *let* exams have so much power over how you feel and instead rewire your brain through positive visualisations and self-belief.

The fact you made it to this day is a testament in itself. We love to believe we haven't done enough, that we're not ready. Unfortunately, or maybe fortunately, you will never be ready. You can only do your best in that exact moment with the resources you've been given and the questions which have been set.

Do your best. Look after yourself. Dare yourself to feel proud.

ADVICE FROM . . . MANINDER (MANI) SACHDEVA

Mani recently graduated from the University of Oxford after studying computer science. He is well known for his incredible fashion sense, lovely personality and for sharing his tips and academic experiences on his YouTube channel.

Know what you know well.

These are the five words I like to remind myself the night before an exam. I often found that the night before I tend to cycle through all the things in my head that I might not know well, or in some cases, at all! Not only does this put me in a state of panic, but the reality is that no amount of last-minute reading of new material will help dwindle this frenzy, or provide me with sufficient information to be able to respond to an exam question at the level that might be required of me. Therefore, as a matter of habit, I find that it's best to focus on what you've revised and what you (hopefully) already know.

The aim is to remain calm and confident, rather than stressing yourself out about all the things that you might not know. This is why I like to ensure that I'm *only* going over the things that I've already revised, in an attempt to reassure myself of the following: *I do know some things, and the things*

I know, I know well. In practice, I do this by steering clear of my exhaustive set of notes or a textbook, and instead, only looking at the consolidated cheat sheet or flashcards that I created. This way, I'm only cementing knowledge I already have, ready to be called upon when I need it in the exam.

I know what you're thinking! What if while going over things I have revised, I realise I don't remember everything? DO NOT PANIC! I REPEAT, DO NOT PANIC! This is the very point of this exercise, as by going over things that you have already previously revised, you are cementing information that you've already exposed your brain to before. By repeating and going over those things again, you're increasing the chances of them staying in your brain! And if you find that while going over things you've already revised, you already know them, that's fantastic! This is the exact confidence boost that you need; it will put you in the right state of mind. Doing this the night before an exam is hitting two birds with one stone (in a totally metaphorical sense, because we are all about those animal rights) going over things one last time, and giving yourself a kick of confidence!

So don't forget – KWYKW!

CHAPTER 12

READY FOR BATTLE: BEFORE, DURING AND AFTER AN EXAM

'Check, check, check.' I ticked the final revision item from my packing list and zipped my pencil case shut, the clear plastic wallet bulging with tools that would help me get one step closer to good grades.

It was 6:30am. Having woken up earlier than usual, my morning was slow. I poured oats into a pan, drizzled almond milk in circles and stirred, just like I did every morning. Because the day you have one of the biggest exams of your life doesn't need to feel like the be-all and end-all moment of your existence. The lead up can and should be calm. Just another day of trying your best.

As I placed my steaming bowl of porridge on the table, I drew out my handy last-minute cheat sheet, brimming with every definition, concept, quote or mark scheme answer that wouldn't stick in my head, but should. Breakfast was almost meditative, testing myself on bites of knowledge between bites of porridge.

On the bus to school, my magic cheat sheet was in my hand again. I could hear friends in front of me chattering nervously about the paper.

'I heard this year's six-marker might be about respiration.'

'Oh my god, I hope not!'

'Why didn't I revise more across the year?!'

The more I tuned into the conversations around me, the more I noticed my knee started bobbing up and down – a nervous tic I developed in times of stress. Did I know the process of respiration well? Oh god, definitely not. My friends were right, the exam boards *did* want us to fail.

I wriggled out my headphones and drowned out the chatter.

Of course, you could always have revised more and maybe you don't know every concept perfectly, but thinking like that on the day of an exam is not a recipe for success.

As the voices of other students faded away, I focused again on my little cheat sheet. Holding it in my hand, it felt like a gift from Past Me – a reminder that I had studied as hard as I could.

When I arrived at school, I had a choice: to get sucked into further conversations about exam fear or to quietly set up my mind.

You see, there's nothing more relatable than exam stress.

And no topic of conversation which interferes with your focus more.

Queueing to enter the exam hall was a sombre process. No one spoke. Each of us clutched clear pencil cases and unlabelled bottles like they were personal lifelines. Occasionally you would meet eyes with a teacher and receive a curt nod of encouragement. Or meet with eyes with a student and offer a half smile of solidarity. There was a tension in the process, arising in a large part from having waited for this moment for so long.

Everyone has their last-last-last minute secret to success and mine was breathing techniques. I'd breathe in for four seconds, hold my breath, and slowly exhale through my nose for six seconds. I refused to let my anxious heartbeat race to a place of stress. I was alive. I was okay.

I repeated words of affirmation to myself in my head: *I have an abundance of time. I am worthy of being successful. I am doing my best.*

And by the time I settled into my allocated seat in the exam hall, I felt ready. Not as though I knew every answer or how to ace the exam, but ready to try my best. And that is always enough.

THE MORNING BEFORE AN EXAM

Is it possible that, after months of studying, countless sheets of revision material, piles of flashcards and long nights cramming, the day has actually arrived? The fateful morning of the real exam? Surreal. Take a moment to breathe and soak in the fact that you made it this far. You should be bloody proud of yourself!

Just like the night before an exam, the morning before is a love letter to your mindset. This is not the time to panic, nor beat yourself up for not trying harder. This is a time to get strategically calm. Productively calm.

I spoke to many high-achieving students about their top tips for the day, and they all fall within one of the facets of '**MORNING**'.

M – Materials. As discussed in the last chapter, the evening before your exam, it is essential to pack the right tools, know the time of your exam on your schedule and the right room to be at. I can vividly remember a student turning up to the GCSE maths calculator exam . . . without a calculator. The school scrabbled to find her one but couldn't. I remember seeing her face fall when she realised she would be doing trigonometry in her head. Make sure you know what you're packing and which items to get rid of. No phones or smartwatches (unfortunately!).

O – Organise early. Wake up at least ten minutes earlier than you normally would. You don't want to feel rushed. Eat a decent breakfast, drink water, pack your bag and soak up a chilled feeling of acceptance. We don't like stress and an abundance of time minimises it.

R – Revise. But don't cram. For peace of mind, look at some last-minute revision resources if it helps you get into the exam mindset. I always had my trusty cheat sheet to hand. If it makes you feel more confident, test yourself on concepts you know.

N – No stress conversations. While supporting a friend the day of the exam is great and going over a last-minute concept with a teacher might be useful, conversations which spiral into fear are unproductive, or even harmful. Half of exam success is mindset. You don't need to hear how confident someone else feels or to listen to them describe in detail how difficult this paper will be. Don't feel guilty for stepping aside and waiting quietly.

I – Inhale, exhale. Whatever mindfulness means to you, focus on being present and calm. I recommend breathing techniques to quieten anxious thoughts and slow your heart rate. Positive visualisation techniques and affirmations are also a last-minute trick for success. As discussed in chapter 10, there are many scientific papers that indicate positive self-affirmation before an exam increases academic performance (and the reverse!). Rather than telling yourself why you're not worthy of good grades, consciously hype yourself up. I can confirm that the person reading this (aka, you) is worthy of good grades.

N – Nice reward later. Visualise yourself after this exam, soaking up free time, hanging out with friends and being proud of yourself. Get motivated by the prospect of smashing it out now.

G – Go for it! You've got this. Realise that you can only do your best in *that* moment, with the questions presented to you, with the revision you've done and with however you feel that day. The acceptance that comes knowing that and trying your best, makes results less important.

Every day that you have an exam, go through the **MORNING** list to yourself again. **M**aterials? Check. **O**rganised and ready to go early? Yes. A bit of chilled **R**evision beforehand and definitely **N**o stressed conversations. **I**nhale and breathe, centering yourself with the reminder of a **N**ice reward later that day. Finally, **G**o for it. Mindset, mindset, mindset. Believing in yourself is half the work.

DURING AN EXAM

Clocks ticking. Pens scribbling. Invigilators walking oh-so-slowly. You think exams are just about knowing the answers? Nope, there's a whole environment around you which contributes to your success. Here are my handy tips to do your best in the exam hall!

Exam success hinges on three main variables:

- Time
- Knowledge
- Mindset

How you attend to these three variables indicates how successful you will be.

Your success in the domain of **knowledge** depends on how efficient your revision has been; **time** and **mindset** are the keys to accessing this knowledge within the exam situation in a way that gets you the marks you want.

Time

This is your constraint. If we all had infinite time, we could mull over our answers, dig into our thought processes and produce more coherent responses. We could write whole books for history essays or recalculate every maths problem until we're Einstein.

But you don't get infinite time.

Some subjects are especially time-constrained. I remember struggling my way through religious studies exams where you had just 30 minutes to fully plan, develop and write a ground-breaking essay.

The harsher, the better

With such limited time, be harsh with yourself. Memorise the allocated time you should spend on each section of the paper. Know where you should be at half time. Calculate the exact time you need to switch to the next question.

But most crucially, be harsher than you need to be. If you know you only have 45 minutes to write an essay, give yourself 40 minutes. If you know you normally need 10 minutes to plan an essay, give yourself only 8. The act of feeling more time-pressured than you are will make you more efficient and crucially leave you time to check through and revise your answers or reattempt questions.

Where are the seconds going?

While focusing on the questions, have a constant awareness of where time is at. As soon as you enter the room, find the clock and get familiar with it. Equally, check if you're allowed to bring a watch into the exam hall. If so, lucky you! The ability to track time on your wrist at a glance away will help you prioritise.

Make it a habit to regularly check in with the clock. Don't let it induce stress. Think of the clock as your friend, encouraging you to use your seconds like gifts.

Mindset

Mindset works in a feedback loop with posture, body language and sense of self-belief. If you enter the room physically terrified, hands shaking and repeating to yourself that you're bound to fail, you just brought that thought one step closer to reality.

Fake it till you make it

There is an art to faking confidence: dare yourself to stand up straight as you walk into the exam hall. Settle yourself into the chair like it's a comfortable throne. Revel in slowly taking out your pen, locating and admiring the clock on the wall and finding humour in how well-orchestrated the exam environment is. This entire show was put on for you. That invigilator there? They're technically here for you. How flattering. The effort to make the room silent? Again, all for you to optimise focus. How kind.

The more you can paint fun stories over what exams are, the easier it is to be confident within them.

I made it a personal goal to smile at every invigilator and even utter them a 'good morning' as I entered the hall. Something about offering warmth made me feel calm, like I was totally unfazed by what was about to happen.

If mindset is the key to unlocking deep knowledge, hone it. Fake yourself calm to make yourself calm.

What story will you tell yourself about the exam hall?

The flow

Yes, you are now a river. And you've got to find your flow. The exam flow is intangible but life-changing. If you've ever experienced exams as an otherworldly experience, you know what I'm talking about. It's being told the time is up and looking up from your exam paper as though remembering for the first time where you are. How strange that a piece of paper can prompt such deep thought and fast processing.

Finding the flow is about attention span and practice. The more practice exam papers you finish without distractions or breaks, the better you become at finding and committing to the flow. The exam flow is internal synergy. It's about moving through the paper methodically and with intention. It's about seeing a key term and having knowledge rush back to you as your pen hits the paper. It's about seeing a word in a language exam that you can't remember the meaning of, but your brain decides to struggle and struggle again to find a potential meaning that works. Flow is about drowning out the sounds around you, not even noticing the door opening or the distant coughing in the exam hall.

Flow can be trainesd through engaging in more frequent deep-processing exercises and using fewer tools which train a short-attention span, like social media. As discussed in previous chapters, you can develop a longer attention span. For example, catch yourself on social media when you notice yourself becoming passive. Engage in long movies without breaking focus or read a book for a few hours. Training a longer attention span makes finding flow easier.

CHEEKY TIP! (Don't tell the exam board)

Sometimes the front of the exam paper is transparent enough to make out the keywords of the first question on the next page. When you're writing your name on the front page, lightly press down and you might be able to read the first question ahead of time. In essay-based exams, this buys you valuable time! If you know the main theme, character or historical event you're going to be asked to write about, as the invigilator is going through procedures before the start of the exam, you can begin thinking about your essay framework. No rules are being broken here! We love thin paper.

Scribble your heart out – no one's judging

Take advantage of your scrap paper or the edges of the exam sheet that you can use for pencil workings you can then rub out. When using revision techniques like making anagrams, using images as knowledge prompts or associating knowledge to objects, little drawings were essential to my recall.

For example, when asked to calculate the speed of a vehicle in a maths or physics problem, the only way I remembered how to do it was through drawing the formula triangle with s (speed), d (distance) and t (time).

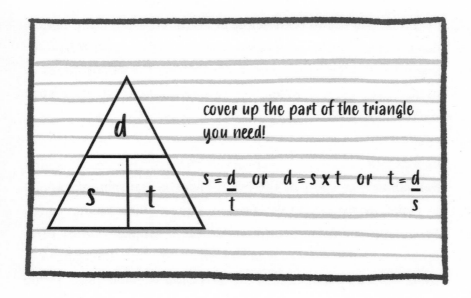

I drew this on the exam paper and, as I had memorised the meaning of letters within it, it was enough to give me the formula I needed! I then quickly rubbed out the pencil lines.

Everyone learns differently. For visual learners, get scribbling!

Help – I don't get the question*

Remember, time is one of the most important variables to consider during an exam. Through practice, you start to recognise if a question is within reach but taking longer than you thought or if you're just wasting time. Develop a system of putting a star next to a question you need to come back to. Then keep working through the paper. The idea is that you can collect marks on questions you *are* confident in and leave these problem questions for later.

However, I remember the sense of dread I felt when I asterisked not one, not two, but five or more questions. Sometimes the exam paper is just so tough that multiple questions need review.

If this is the case, don't panic. Be methodical and calm. Review the questions you starred, beginning with the one that feels most accessible. Dig into it. Use any keywords in the question as prompts to Blurt your knowledge on the side of the paper.

I remember doing this during a biology exam. I had no idea what the question was asking. It was about an enzyme I had never seen before in a brand new context. I calmly drew an asterisk next to the question and decided to come back to it later for review.

The next time I approached it, I began writing everything I knew about enzymes on the sides of the paper in pencil. Any keywords that came to mind. Common enzyme functions. Key characteristics of enzymes. All of it. It was only then that I started to understand the question better. The question wasn't just asking me about enzymes, it was asking me about *proteins* and protein structure, because enzymes are proteins.

If you're feeling stuck, use your background knowledge to help bring context to a question which seems foreign. Always ground vague questions in foundations you *do* know.

And if it's a maths question, hey, at least writing down formulas or doing the first few lines of working will usually get you a few marks!

Exams can be kinda ... beautiful?

Hear me out on this one. Isn't there something cathartic about Blurting out all this knowledge you've been packing into your head for months? You enter a flow zone where it's just you and the paper. You and the knowledge and time. On the surface, it's just a bunch of students sitting at desks, silent apart from the hushed murmur of pens on paper. But each student is deep in their own little world, constructing intricate lines of thought in essays or solving maths problems they've quite literally never seen before using only what they know. Each student is engaging in a process of world-building where they turn prompts on a piece of paper into elaborate models of thought. Though each student conducts the exam alone, they are connected to every other student in that room with a sense of solidarity.

Of course, exams are bloody tough. But finding some kind of high-level beauty in them, as though you were looking back at this moment in 50 years, minimises the power they have over you.

AFTER AN EXAM

Laugh. Cry. Eat a doughnut (or five). I'm a firm believer that you should reward yourself after hard work. Whether the exam felt like it went well or not, you did your best.

People often aren't comforted by the idea of 'doing your best' because in their opinion, your best can always be better. It feels like there is always more you could've done, more revision resources you could've made, more hours spent studying. But that's not the point of the phrase. The idea is not to reach a new personal best. It is to simply put your greatest effort into the given questions, at that moment, however you feel that day. *That* is your best. Your best given the exact circumstances of that moment. All anyone can ask of you is that you revised your socks off and committed.

So be proud. Hold your head high as you leave the exam hall, even if you struggled or froze. Stop overthinking the questions you think you should've known or second-guessing your answers.

I want to once again focus on what you have just achieved. You're just a young person going through some of the hardest moments of your life – emotionally, physically and in terms of personal growth. You are in a system which requires you to not just learn for fun but to learn so you can be given the keys to your future. You are being graded in a standardised way which does not reflect everyone's true potential. That is an immense amount of pressure. No one can downplay that what you just did was brave. With all the people watching you from the sidelines, you stared the exam in the face and just did it.

Top three BEST things to do after an exam

1. Twitter. Never again in your life will you have the *joy* of exam memes specific to that exam. I was never an avid Twitter user. I didn't even have an account. But I lapped up every relatable joke like it was made for me.

   Search up the hashtag of the exam you took and enter a gold mine of comedic brilliance. Watch young people around the country tear apart the exam boards, make memes out of hard questions and feel a collective sense of solidarity. I've never felt as part of something as I did when I read exam memes.

2. Anything mind-numbing. You know those shows that don't require you to think? The ones you can turn on and they make you dissolve away? Those are everything after an exam. I would steer clear of TV series I'd get addicted to, but reruns of *Friends* or the drama of *Love Island* was enough to forget my previous stress.

3. Write in a journal. Though reflecting on your exam might sound like your worst nightmare, running through your thoughts is calming. If you are beating yourself up about what you could've done better, expressing your thoughts helps you rationalise them.

What if the exam didn't go well?

Flashback to my A level biology exam in Year 13. The exam board that year was cruel. AQA, you've made an enemy.

Rather than a 15-page paper of standard formatting and questions, our A level exam was a thick booklet nearing 50 pages in length. Every practice paper I'd ever done felt irrelevant. The exam flow and timings I had honed flew out the window. I felt anger rising through the panic. How was this even allowed? I flicked through endless low-mark questions seemingly without end.

But of course, I had to bloody try. I couldn't let the exam board win. So I filled my margins with workings and tackled the exam head on. The top of my paper was decorated with squiggles, diagrams and memory prompts.

You can't imagine the stress I felt when I looked up at the clock to see I'd used half my time. I was two solid pages away from the midway staples of the paper: I was behind. Time seemed to fall through my hands like sand. My heart started pounding. I frantically asterisked question after question that felt too time-heavy to understand. I flicked through the never-ending paper feeling like every hope I'd had for getting into a good university was falling away. In my panic, I started breathing too quickly, not reading questions properly and therefore struggling to get a footing on any of them.

The exam was a blur. I've never experienced such a wave of disappointment as when the invigilator told us that time was up. I hadn't finished the paper. I didn't even check through. The pages felt like lead as I closed them. I hardly heard what the invigilators said because I was so out of it.

The second I got out of the exam hall, I burst into tears. My biology teacher, the one who sacrificed her lunchtimes to help me pass these exams, was waiting outside. I couldn't face her. I had never felt so much like I'd failed.

By the time I got in the car with my mum, I was sobbing. Red-faced, ugly-cry sobbing. I cursed myself over and over for how poorly I'd handled the timing of the paper. I cursed meditation and mindfulness for not helping me when I really needed them.

What I mean to say is, it happens.

There will be bad exams. There will be bad papers. There will be moments you stare yourself in the face and feel like all hope for your future is fading before your eyes.

But maybe that's the point of it all, this whole exam system. It teaches you to be resilient. I had to learn the hard way not to define my self-worth in the results of that paper. At the end of the day, I did my best. Not my best performance, but my best effort under that time-pressure and those mean questions.

In the end, the exam board ended up having extremely low grade boundaries and I was still able to achieve a good grade after making many mistakes. Odds are, if you found an exam tough, others did too. The grade boundaries will reflect the difficulty of the exam and sometimes it might save you.

When a paper was bad, this is what you do

Give yourself an allotted time to feel sorry for yourself. Get it out of your system. Dedicate yourself to processing however stressed you feel rather than suppressing your feelings and moving straight onto revision for the next exam. Cry if you need to. Call a friend if it helps. Burn your revision notes to ashes (okay, maybe not). Anything.

And then move on. Recentre yourself. Remind yourself of what you're grateful for, that you're brilliant and that you're also just human.

Rather than running over every question again in your head, bring your focus to the next subject or exam.

THE NEXT EXAM

After rewarding yourself and processing however the exam went, draw your attention to whatever's next. To reduce friction to getting started, I recommend laying out the revision resources you need on your desk or bed beforehand so it feels easier to pick up when you're tired!

Once again, strategise. Don't waste time rereading or highlighting. Return to the section on revision techniques for a refresher on how to make your revision SAAD and effective.

Optimise timetabling to ensure you can cover everything you want to before the next exam.

By this point, you're a pro. Keep going. You've got this.

FINISHED?

Or maybe that was your last exam? CONGRATULATIONS!

I am writing these words from a little library in Seoul, South Korea and I am *infusing* these lines with imaginary confetti. All the people silently working in this library don't even realise they're at an impromptu party. Imagine celebrations raining from the pages. You deserve it.

Exam season is a marathon and after marathons you deserve rest. And snacks. And a whole bloody holiday in the Maldives. All that revision and hard work paid off, even if it doesn't feel like it yet. Go celebrate!

ADVICE FROM . . . JACK EDWARDS

Jack studied English literature at Durham University after achieving all A*s in his A levels. Beyond this academic overview, he is a self-proclaimed book nerd and avid hummus lover. Here he shared his most essential tips for smashing the exams!

Telling someone "remember to breathe" during an exam feels almost as redundant as telling a fish to swim . . . but it's actually really great advice! An exam is a high-pressure, high-intensity situation, and often incredibly overwhelming. So, let's break down that abstract idea "remember to breathe" into something more practical. If you find yourself starting to panic, place one hand on the desk in front of you and trace it slowly with the index finger of your other hand. As you move up each finger, inhale. As you move back down again, exhale. Focus on this activity with intentionality, and take back control of your breathing. Hopefully this quick activity will help you to regain your composure and calm your nerves, so you can get on with smashing that exam without the intrusion of anxious thoughts.

During an exam in essay-based subjects, make sure you spend some time planning your answer before you start writing. This will help you to structure your argument with a clear focus, as well as assisting you in organising your time. An exam-marker once told me that whenever she saw a student had written a plan before their answer, she subconsciously expected a more thought-out essay. That's the best first-impression you could ever make! Write this plan in your answer booklet above your essay, and lightly cross it out with a single, neat line at the end. It's helpful for you *and* for the examiner – a win-win!

After an exam ends, it's almost too tempting to dissect your answers, compare with friends and attempt to figure out how well you did (or didn't) do. However, this is kind of self-destructive. Actually . . . it's *incredibly* self-destructive. Instead, make sure you have a concrete plan for the moment you finish the exam. Allow yourself to unwind and recover properly and be assured in yourself before you hear other people's interpretations. I would always plan to do exercise immediately after an exam, whether that was going for a run or going to the gym, so that I could focus on something else and release some energy. So, when you're planning for that exam, spare a thought for what you're going to do once it's over. It's something to look forward to and also a chance to recalibrate your thoughts.

CHAPTER 13

THE FUTURE YOU'RE STUDYING FOR

It seems only natural to finish with a chapter about what happens when this is all over. School is temporary. That stack of flashcards on your desk won't always be there (unless it's just *that* aesthetic). You won't always have revision to do. There won't be notes to make every day. End of chapter tests won't be sprung on you every month of later life.

If you're still in the lower years of school, I hope this chapter reassures you that it's fine to experiment, to shift and change your perceptions of what you want to study and the job you want to pursue as you progress through school. For now, you have the luxury of practising different study techniques until you master them, finding out how you work best, dreaming big about your future life and, most importantly, enjoying your summer holidays!

Though this time of your life sets you up for everything after, it is short-lived. Suddenly, you'll be looking back and feeling so much gratitude that you worked as hard as you did. You'll think back to the days you chose to study that extra hour instead of going on your phone. You'll be grateful you picked up books that helped you learn how to optimise your time. You'll be thankful for instilling good habits that look after your mental health.

I know I am.

As I write this, I am studying at the university of my dreams, where I gained entry due to the A*s I worked so hard for. Fifteen-year-old me would probably look at where I am right now and sob. I cannot believe how enriched I feel. I want to know everything about everything, whether it's in a text-book or not. I don't attach myself to grades in the way I used to. I don't feel stressed about academic life because I've learned the systems I need to optimise my time. My world perspective is ever-growing, helped along by meeting people from so many different countries, learning about other cultures and by reading.

I am Future Jade, right now. I cannot be more grateful for everything Past Me at secondary school did to get me here.

But even so, finding my path to where I am right now was not as straightforward as you might think. Welcome to the messiness of me working out my academic stepping stones and some realisations I've had along the way. This book is a study guide, and so much of your studies is guided by your plans for the future. Whether you know exactly what you want to study and pursue, or have absolutely no idea, you are valid.

In my life, I have been two types of person: the one who knows with absolute certainty what job they want to have in the future and strives with every ounce of themselves to achieve it, and the scattered existential mess with no bloody clue. I hope my story helps someone who is feeling lost. As you look towards the rest of your life, I'll try to impart some of the older-sibling wisdom that I wish I'd had.

I DON'T KNOW WHAT I WANT TO DO WITH THE REST OF MY LIFE!

Saturday. The alarm clock rang a familiar 6:30am and I dragged myself out of bed like I had done every weekend for the last three years. I scrunched my hair into a low-hanging ponytail, pulled on horse-riding jodhpurs and made it to the stables for 8am, looking forward to a free riding session in exchange for a day's work. The following week was half term and I was going to spend it at a local animal rescue centre, who had taken months of convincing to let a fifteen-year-old girl volunteer with them. Little did they know that I was accustomed to balancing bales of hay on a wheelbarrow, ardently mucking out animals and taking just 30-minute breaks in freezing cold English winters to eat my lunch.

I spent most of my teenage years wanting to be a vet.

Becoming a vet is no easy feat. Besides the need to study sciences and mathematics intensely at school, getting into veterinary universities requires six to ten weeks of work experience in various animal-related establishments. By the age of 17, I had spent almost every school holiday working at kennels, catteries, animal rescues or shadowing veterinary practices. I even got myself work experience at London Zoo. In my free time, I would go to the library and max out the limit of books, reading about the anatomy of horse hooves or the eyesight of dogs. I was dedicated.

People at school knew me as 'the girl who wants to be a vet' – it was tied up with my identity – and even though my school had never had a student accepted into veterinary school, I believed that with enough work, I could break the trend.

When I attended talks about future career plans and saw an overwhelming number of my friends raising their hand to indicate they didn't know what to do with their future, I could not relate to them. I had my goal and I was working towards it.

However, the more time I spent with vets – watching surgeries or sorting medicine cabinets – the more acutely I felt a sense of not belonging. I don't know if it was the sterile environment, hearing about how overworked many of the vets were, the long hours you spend on your feet or that I had romanticised the job from the many veterinary TV shows I had watched (I blame you, *Bondi Vet!*), but I began to wonder if the job was really for me. I continued getting work experience, studying chemistry, biology and maths, and researching universities but I felt a growing sense of fear.

I didn't want to have to admit that I wasn't keen on the job anymore. It felt like I'd be disappointing my family, who had supported the dream for so long, and my science teachers, who believed that with enough work, I could achieve the grades to get into vet school. I had dedicated so many hours of work to getting the experience I needed, so, especially when I couldn't explain how I now knew this was not the path I wished to pursue, I didn't have the heart to tell anyone I had changed my mind.

Suddenly, I had gone from someone who knew with certainty where they wanted to go and the exact steps necessary to get there, to feeling lost, with no sense of who I was anymore. What did I even enjoy? What did I want to spend all my time doing? How could I make my teachers and parents proud if I didn't train to be a vet?

To make the situation worse, I decided to put off the decision and take a gap year. There was no reputable internship lined up, no promise of an Oxford degree thereafter and certainly no more qualifications coming my way in a year of working and exploring myself. It was the first decision I made in my life truly for me, not to get certain grades or under pressure from teachers or peers. I faced up to the fact that I didn't know what I wanted to do with my life and decided that venturing out of the bubble of the education system was a pretty cool first step to working it out.

Taking a gap year was everything I needed in order to learn about the world as not fixed but abundant in opportunities and nuance. On my solo backpacking travels, I met adults who had lived four or five successful careers, learning about themselves in the process. I met people who studied what they loved, only to pivot into a totally different career they equally loved. I realised that life is not just about what you work as or how heavy your pay cheque is. I learned that you will never just be defined by your job. Work is a role you play to survive, contribute to the world and hopefully bring fulfilment to your life, but it is not everything.

DEFINE YOUR VALUES

If you are looking to your working life with a sense of dread, I invite you not to worry about specific routes. As terrifying as it feels to live in uncertainty, it gives you breathing room to find the right space for you, one which might not even exist yet.

The question of how to spend the entire rest of your life is terrifying – and unnecessary. The concept of one dream job is a directive of a past in which adults assumed one position in one company for most of their working life. We live in a very different world now, in which careers shift, roles are more fluid and working culture is dynamic, especially with the influence of technology.

Nonetheless, the question persists throughout our lives: 'What do you want to be when you're older?' If that question fills you with dread, I reassure you that not knowing, changing your mind, having a million different career ideas (or zero!) is absolutely okay. Not least because this question is fundamentally flawed. **The question of *who* you want to be when you're older should not be about your means of making money.** You are going to be a full, incredible person defined by the colours of your personality, the relationships you cultivate and your approach to life – no matter what your future occupation.

What is far more important than the specific job title is defining your personal values. This you can do at any age. What are the values that make up you as a person? What features of your working life will make you feel fulfilled? For example, is it likely to be meeting new people every day under the value of 'connection' or working in a team because you value 'community'? Job satisfaction is not necessarily about the amount you earn, nor how cool it looks on your LinkedIn profile. Instead, it's about knowing yourself as a person and the kind of impact you want to have in the world.

The more I realise the fundamentals of what my day-to-day life needs to look like to make me feel fulfilled, the less stress I experience about defining a concrete career path. When people ask me what I want to do, I remind myself that not having a specific answer does not mean I am lazy. I am just still working it out.

The world is dynamic and shifting. The more you can hone your skillset in whatever you love, while cultivating your values, the better equipped you will be to find a job that fulfils you.

But I get that defining fluffy values feels unsatisfying, especially with expectations to earn money and carve out a sustainable life.

In a world that demands the concrete, here is a simple exercise to help you define what you want to do.

YOU'RE ABOUT TO CHANGE YOUR LIFE: ODYSSEY PLANS

This technique, developed from the Design Your Life course at Stanford University, was presented to me in my first year of university. It is a framework for viewing your life as abundant. It invites you to treat your life as something under your control – you are the 'designer'.

I recently sent this Odyssey Plan exercise to my younger brother who is in sixth form when he was experiencing a moment of crisis. He nodded at the words and said it looked helpful. And then didn't do it. I laughed because it's just so human. If you're reading this chapter and you are tempted to say that you'll try this exercise another day, I want to remind you that 'another day' will probably never come. If you're struggling with thinking about your future, go grab a pen and take ten minutes to do this exercise. This moment could change the course of your life.

You will envision your life in three ways under different criteria. Detail everything you can about how you see your life – from your day-to-day work, the country you're living in, relationships and interests. Be bold, big and clear.

1) **Write down what your life will look like in five years if you continue on the path you're on right now.** Even if that path seems hazy, extrapolate what you are currently studying or thinking about. For me in Year 11, that would have been veterinary medicine. I saw myself graduating vet school, entering

the training phase of life as a veterinary surgeon and likely living in the UK. I envisioned myself having many friends who were probably also vets. I would not have much free time and likely be working emergency shifts at night but I'm sure I would still be doing yoga and meditation. I like to think I'd be happy.

2) **Write down what your life will look in five years if you choose a different, but realistic alternative path.** This could be one you have thought about but do not think is feasible, for whatever reason. For example, entertain the idea of changing your A level subjects or pivoting the type of work experience you pursue. For me, this was taking a gap year, re-evaluating my life and what I wanted to study. I've always loved literature, humanities and business just as much as sciences, so in this Odyssey Plan, I would dare myself to imagine studying one of these subjects instead. I imagined the kind of university I would go to, where I would live and the job that would follow. For example, setting up my own start-up company, or non-profit. Maybe working in journalism if I pursued writing or pivoting back to science if my studies led me there.

3) **Write down what your life will look like in five years if money and outside expectations of you didn't matter.** This could be anything. Get wild. Get crazy. Would you be presenting a cooking show? Reading books all day long? Travelling the world? Becoming a yoga teacher? Or making videos? What are the hobbies you are doing day-to-day and where do you live?

This process is really important because it's guaranteed to make you view yourself as less trapped in your current reality. It shows you that there are always other options, even when it doesn't feel like it. The final prompt is especially powerful in showing you what you *really* want to be doing: can any parts of this come true in your actual life? Sometimes wild ideas are the best at allowing you to question yourself and your current path.

If you still don't know what you want to do post-school, that's okay. You get to have the fun of being a scientist in your own life. Every choice is an experiment towards finding where you want to be. Choose something. Commit to it. You'll soon find out if it's right or not and you'll probably learn something in the process.

Remember, the more you study and work hard now, the more options you are giving Future You!

REACH FOR THE SKIES – EVEN IF THE SKIES REJECT YOU

Through a lifetime of being told which opportunities are for you (and which aren't!), of seeing people that look like you (or don't!) occupying certain spaces and of carving a reality based on what you think you deserve, you start to place limits on your life. Certain universities, subjects of study, jobs and opportunities begin to feel out of reach, as though pursuing them is asking for a piece of a pie that was never baked for you.

As we get closer to finishing school, we need to think about our lives through an admittedly realistic lens, but also a bold one. Applying for universities and jobs is already terrifying; the danger is we can trick ourselves into choosing what feels easier, or safer. We look at our past and who we are and try to fit ourselves like a puzzle piece into somewhere we see a close fit. The idea of aiming higher than what is immediately in front of us requires imagination and resilience, which is difficult to find without robust support systems.

And yet, I want you to think big and view yourself as worthy of fighting for the places you want to go when all this studying is done. If the people around you ask you to shrink into easily achievable spaces, I implore you to challenge them.

In the whole history of my state school, only a handful people made it to Oxford and Cambridge universities – the world-renowned UK institutions of dreams. Everyone knew about them, of course. From the long Hogwarts-like halls to the gorgeous black capes students donned during exam season, they were institutions of mystery and magic, reserved for a wealthy few who were the geniuses of the world. Or so I thought. All I knew about Oxbridge was the stereotypes. Most people I knew did not even consider applying. I felt like that for a long time.

My parents are not very academic and knew nothing about the university system. My dad left school when he was 16 and my mum picked up vocational school in the Netherlands. I never visited a university until sixth form and honestly had no idea how it worked. The thought of applying anywhere filled me with anxiety and if it hadn't been for YouTubers at university sharing their experience, I would have had no conception of what daily university life was like.

My story is not one of woe, nor very dramatic or unique. I have lived such a privileged life compared to many others. Though my parents are not academic they always supported me in following whatever dreams I had for myself. But this lack of knowledge about universities gave me a feeling of imposter syndrome when it came to applying. I loved learning. I knew

I was academic. And yet I couldn't help be influenced by the dreams of those around me. None of my close friends were applying to Oxbridge – even friends who were, in my eyes, clever enough for it. The thought of the interview process was too terrifying and the idea of not fitting into the grandness of the place was equally off-putting.

I made myself apply to Oxbridge for a few reasons. Firstly, in Year 12 I got into a one-week summer school at Cambridge for state school students. It was an incredibly enriching experience which changed my perceptions of Oxbridge. Secondly, some of my A level teachers became my friends and were willing to challenge me to apply. My god, did I love them.

Though my school didn't offer formal Oxbridge training, my biology teacher took it upon herself to research Oxbridge and stay with me at lunchtimes, teaching me what I could potentially expect from the interview. Her kindness was above and beyond what the school itself could offer, seeing as there wasn't an army of students applying.

I read every online resource I could about writing personal statements, polishing that all-important document for the early application deadline. I reached out to current students at Oxbridge on social media and even became friends with a few on YouTube. It helped me start to normalise the institutions and dare myself to imagine myself there.

The day I received the offer of an interview, I sobbed.

Two other girls in my year group had also applied to Oxbridge and both had interviews too. It was a total schoolwide success. The news spread like wildfire. Teachers I hardly knew congratulated me in the corridors.

I went to the library almost every day and inhaled books. I wanted to know everything and anything I could about my subject in preparation for the dreaded interview. I didn't know what to wear. I borrowed one of my mum's 'professional' outfits to make myself feel proper.

The two-day interview process involved living at the university (for free!), answering very reasonable questions about my subject in interviews with multiple professors, and overall discerning whether or not I'd be a good fit. I stayed in Brasenose College, Oxford. This in itself was an unimaginable dream. I had my own room in one of the most famous cities in England. I could peer out onto the cobbled streets, run my hands over windowsills touched by great academics of the past and geek out over libraries upon libraries of books. That weekend, I met students from all over the world, brought together by a passion for learning. I had the most fascinating conversations and it made me start to realise that all the people applying were just people too. Regardless of what preparation they might have had, we were all just students who liked learning. There were students from all walks of life and far more came from state schools than I initially imagined. My fears were irrational and driven by harmful stereotypes.

The interviews were terrifying and yet, dare I say it, fun. How often do you get to speak to one of the world-leading academics in a niche area of your subject? I was living a once-in-a-lifetime moment and I wrote down every little detail in a notebook so I could tell my family about the experience. I left each interview knowing that I had done my best. That was enough.

I returned home from Oxford feeling like my world had just shifted. Why had I been so terrified to apply? If I hadn't just taken the chance, I would not have been able to live such an enriching weekend, nor meet the wonderful people that I did. I thought about the stereotypes I had believed and how crippling they are. Oxbridge *is* achievable, no matter your background.

As I babbled away to my parents at dinner time about everything from the gorgeous architecture to the incredible people, I started doing what I had never dared allow myself to before: I imagined myself at Oxford University.

In January, I was rejected.

Ha. Oh, life is cruel. After taking hundreds of thousands of viewers on my YouTube channel on the crazy application journey, not to mention letting my teachers and parents live this fantasy experience with me, any hope I had of getting in was ripped from under my feet. It was a confirmation of all my fears. I started asking myself how on earth I had thought myself worthy enough of attending one of the best universities in the world. Every time I didn't understand something at school, it bitterly confirmed I probably would not even achieve Oxford-worthy grades anyway. I wanted to shrink into myself, promising myself not to dream so big in the future. My academic confidence plummeted.

Regret is an interesting thing. At that moment in time, regret reared its ugly head in the form of shame and embarrassment. I regretted raising my ambitions. I regretted trying hard. More than anything, I regretted taking so many people on the journey with me.

But regret is temporary. In that snippet of short-term outlook, I regretted it all. Today, I am writing this with the long-term perspective of sheer gratitude for not only that application but that rejection.

As my good friend and YouTuber IbzMo says, 'Rejection is redirection.'

I was redirected onto an incredible path. Through a life-changing gap year of self-discovery and growth, investing in my online platforms and finding a revolutionary, world-renowned international university far more suited to my ambitions in life, I set myself on a course that I could never regret.

That's the thing: you can never regret aiming high. Dreams *should* scare you because they are bigger than your fears. Dreams should push you to reimagine the life that was set out for you.

That rejection taught me an incredible amount. I firmly believe that everything happens for a reason, one which we may not currently see. We must push ourselves to do our best but the truly best outcomes in life are often not ones we had foreseen.

So if you are considering your future life plans after school, I beg you: think big. Even if there are seemingly huge roadblocks in your path – be it financially, academically, circumstantially, mental health-wise and more – still dream big. You are more than your circumstances. Luck exists. Life can be serendipitous in helping you achieve what you wish, if only you work hard enough and dare yourself to believe you are good enough.

I don't care if you fail. You shouldn't either. Failure is a tool for further success and teaches you more than success ever could. Failing is a sign you challenged yourself sufficiently. It is a moment to smile at yourself and say, I'm so glad I tried.

Whether challenging yourself means taking that gap year and solo travelling, setting up a business, applying to a dream-big university, aiming for a high-profile career, applying to competitive apprenticeships, retaking your A levels or simply taking an academic subject you *know* will take hard work to succeed in, instil in yourself a belief that you are capable.

If rejection is redirection, you first need to define that direction. Find mentors. Invest in yourself. And position your initial direction firmly reaching for the skies and beyond. Whatever comes of it, you will be proud of yourself.

YOU MADE IT!

Whatever your next steps, you made it. Take a moment to breathe in and breathe out. Smile to yourself. Through optimising your time, looking after your mental health and aiming high for your future, you made it through a bloody tough system. Why do I have the urge to give you a hug?

There's no specific reward for defeating the game of school – your grades don't really begin to tell the whole story – but I hope you recognise it's no easy feat. You will always look back on this time with admiration and gratitude for yourself. Take a moment to reflect on everything you've done to support your future life.

You deserve every single one of your dreams.

PUT IT IN PRACTICE:

- Complete your Odyssey Plan for the next three years with a realistic outline, Plan B and wild imaginative dream.
- What are you aiming for? Why? Do you naturally place limitations on your dreams?

ADVICE FROM . . . EVE CORNWELL

Hello everyone! My name is Eve and I'm nearing the end of my two-year graduate scheme (or, as lawyers call it, my 'training contract'). I graduated from the University of Bristol in 2018 and completed my post graduate Legal Practice Course in 2019 (a qualification you require to become a solicitor in England and Wales). So you could say I'm quite well versed in both student and graduate life!

Jade invited me to write about Life Beyond School, which admittedly, as a 17-year-old, took me a while to understand – there is a life beyond your studies? Um? So you mean to say that we have life beyond exams, grades and qualifications? I know, it's pretty wild.

Your 'career' and 'future' are probably the most common buzzwords used in classrooms, alongside the classic stomach turning 'oh so what do you want to do?' rolled out every Christmas. I'm a huge believer in remaining as open-minded as possible about your future. The job I am doing now (training at a corporate law firm in London) is not what I would have told you I would be doing four years ago, and yet I love it.

The great thing is, we no longer live in a society where having one linear career is the norm. Instead, empowered by diverse skill-sets, we can shape-shift between degree disciplines, industries and job titles. Even myself, studying in a traditionally vocational subject such as law, I considered many non-law opportunities at graduation.

At our core, we are less defined by our degrees or qualifications, but we draw our value and worth from our mindset, core values and approach. Ambition, resilience and positivity will make you successful – and if you have those, you will continue to grow and re-route until you are on the right path. Trust in yourself and your potential, and the big decisions become less scary.

I want to end the book with one parting message:

No matter how much revision you do, no matter what your grades are, and no matter what your friends, teachers, parents or family think of you – you will always be enough.

Success means being proud of yourself for doing your best. So, I wish you success. I wish you all of it. I wish that you can look yourself in the mirror and pat yourself on the back no matter what that piece of paper says on results day. I wish you the success of feeling like you're enough. Because you are.

Jade x

BIBLIOGRAPHY

Allen, D., *Getting Things Done: the Art of Stress-free Productivity* (Piatkus, 2015)

Bor, D., *The Ravenous Brain: How the New Science of Consciousness Explains Our Insatiable Search for Meaning* (Basic Books, 2012)

Cirillo, F., *The Pomodoro Technique: The Life-Changing Time-Management System* (Virgin Books, 2018)

Clear, J., *Atomic Habits* (Random House Business, 2018)

Dispenza, J., *Breaking the Habit of Being Yourself* (Hay House UK, 2012)

Duhigg, C., *The Power of Habit: why we do what we do, and how to change* (Random House, 2013)

Ebbinghaus, H., *Memory. A Contribution to Experimental Psychology* (Dover, 1885). See also "The Forgetting Curve" (https://www.psychestudy.com/ cognitive/memory/ebbinghaus-forgetting-curve)

Hebb, D., *The Organization of Behavior: A Neuropsychological Theory* (Wiley, 1949)

Koch, R., *The 80/20 Principle: The Secret of Achieving More with Less* (Currency, 1999)

Kosslyn, S., "The Science of Learning: Mechanisms and Principles" in S. Kosslyn & B. Nelson, *Building the Intentional University* (MIT Press, 2017)

Maratos, F., "The UK education system needs to change to encourage greater health and wellbeing" (https://fenews.co.uk)

Mobley, M., R.B. Slaney & K.G. Rice, "Cultural validity of the Almost Perfect Scale" (*Journal of Counseling Psychology*, 2005, 52/4, 629–39)

Murre, J.M.J. & J. Dros, "Replication and Analysis of Ebbinghaus' Forgetting Curve" (https://doi.org/10.1371/journal.pone.0120644)

Norton, M.I., D. Mochon & D. Ariely, "The IKEA Effect: When Labor Leads to Love" (*Journal of Consumer Psychology*, 2012, 22, no. 3, 453–460)

Pavlina, S., "How to Make Accurate Time Estimates" (https://StevePavlina.com)

Sinek, S., *Start With Why: How Great Leaders Inspire Everyone* (Penguin, 2011)

Swider, B., D. Harari, et al, "The Pros and Cons of Perfectionism, According to Research" (*Harvard Business Review*, Dec 27, 2018: https://hbr.org/2018/12/the-pros-and-cons-of-perfectionism-according-to-research)

Walker, M., Why We Sleep (Allen Lane, 2017)

THINGS TO EXPLORE

Books:
Taking Up Space: *The Black Girl's Manifesto For Change* by Chelsea Kwakye and Ore
    Ogunbiyi
The Uni-Verse by Jack Edwards (super helpful for anyone thinking of going to university!)

Podcasts:
Akimbo – Seth Godin
Happy Place – Fearne Cotton
The Wooden Spoon

Educational YouTube Channels:
Biology Carol (my incredible biology teacher from A Levels!)
Crash Course
Khan Academy
TED

Study YouTubers:
Ali Abdaal
Ehis Ilozobhie
Eve Bennett
Holly Gabrielle
Jack Edwards
Ruby Granger
Thomas Frank
Vee Kativhu

Mental Health Support:
Mind – www.mind.org.uk
Nightline Association – www.nightline.ac.uk
Samaritans – www.samaritans.org

GLOSSARY

80/20 Principle: The idea that 80% of the final output comes from only 20% of the input. Identify which parts of your study habits generate the most benefit to your grades and optimise for them!

Active Recall: Rather than passively reading information in front of you, active recall means pulling knowledge from your memory when prompted. For example, answering questions without your notes or summarising something from memory.

Association: Making connections between new things that you are learning and your existing knowledge. For example, finding similarities between words in a new language and yours.

Blurting: A highly effective revision technique where you 'blurt' down on paper everything you can remember from a subject or topic from memory. Write yourself prompt words if necessary.

Desirable Difficulty: This means making your revision progressively harder to test your knowledge. Focus on areas which are more difficult rather than covering what you already know.

Fixed Mindset: The idea that our abilities and intelligence cannot be changed, such as believing that you are 'naturally not good at maths'.

Growth Mindset: The idea that our abilities change with time and work, such as believing that you don't understand a maths question yet but you can and you will with enough practice. This mindset is useful to approach mistakes as a point of learning.

MARCKS: A useful acronym to learn from the mistakes you made on past papers to guide your future revision. Count the number of times you lost a mark because of each of these! (Maths error, Application, Read the question, Communication, Knowledge and Statements).

Mark scheme: This document contains the answers to a past paper and is used to mark your work. They are amazing tools to learn from because they tell you how to word your answers, why you've gone wrong and what the exam boards are looking for!

Pomodoro Technique: Set a 25-minute timer and focus on only one task. Then reward yourself with a 5-minute break. This is a useful technique to help structure your time, beat procrastination and enhance deep focus.

Spaced Repetition: To combat the way that humans naturally forget information over time, spaced repetition means reviewing information at slowly increasing intervals to boost your memory back up to 100%. For example, going over a flashcard set on Day 1, Day 3 and Day 6 after first learning it.

Specification: A document created for every subject by your exam board which lists all the things you need to know for the exam. This is very useful to guide your revision!

The Fudge Ratio: This useful calculation helps you make better estimates for how long tasks take you. Simply divide how long a task took you by how long you thought it would take. From now on, multiply your estimates by this number for more accurate planning and timetables!

INDEX

ACKNOWLEDGEMENTS

I was tempted to give my first thank you to AQA — the exam board who made my life enough of a hell that I was inspired enough to talk about it back in 2017, but I'm not sure how my parents would feel.

So, I guess it's only right to start by thanking the two humans who made me Me.

Mum, thank you for loving me and Folk with every ounce of your being. Thank you for teaching me how deep a mother's love can be, for introducing me to mindfulness, and for always being my biggest cheerleader, or should I say, my curly tigereyewarrior. Your vulnerability is rare, and I cherish you every day.

Dad, you're the reason I eat porridge and recite inspirational quotes in every other breath. Your ferocious love and unwavering optimism inspire me every day. Maybe now that you're reading this in print, you'll go take a break. Rest is productive, mate.

To Folkert, Folkie, Folk, Follik. You make me want to be a better older sister every day. I might not have chosen you as family, but I'd choose you over and over as a best friend. Your hugs are unmatched, and your vibes are immaculate. I adore you boi. Now, go revise.

Charlotte, now *you* I did choose as family. I'm glad I pulled your hair as a toddler and held on. I'll be holding on for the rest of our lives. Keep being soft, Pisces Twin.

Sue, when I was a child, you made words feel like worlds. Thank you for inspiring my love of reading and for being my second mum. One day, I want to be as kind as you.

For my beloved wider family who hold half of me permanently with them in the north of the Netherlands. *Ik hou van juillie*. For my family of friends who helped raise me; for Linnea in all your strength and deep love; Jeanette for your warm smile; Paul for being a warm father-figure.

One of my biggest thank yous must go to Mrs Greenslade, Biology Carol, the true revision queen who made me feel like I was capable of anything. Thank you for teaching me how to Blurt, for believing I could get into University of Oxford (screw them!), and for being more than a teacher, but a friend. I will always be beyond grateful for how you positively impacted my life.

For all the incredible teachers who went above and beyond in secondary school — Mrs McCullough, Mrs Rentflejsz, Mrs Dobbs, Mrs Saunders, Mrs Walton, Mr Tarrant, Mrs Harris, Mrs Nuttycombe, Mr Wellman, and Mrs Vaughan.

Amelia, I'm glad we bonded over hating graphics. I would never have survived school (or learned to wear flared trousers) if not for you. Rhiannon, you are sunshine personified; thank you for your yellow. Nemra, you will always be my Bus Buddy; now that it's in print, our bus adventures are immortal. Ceri, thank you for being a boldly loyal friend and for doing the best worm after too much goon. Nara, thank you for your creativity, overflowing warmth and talent for scrap books. Trishna, for being my Maths Buddy. Abby, for making Thursday volunteering the best time of the week. Yasmin, Maddie, Maeve, Emily, and all the other school friends who are the context behind me being happy in the setting of this book. You all shaped me, and I will always be grateful.

Lara, for understanding me in one look, and for being one of the strongest women I know. Mama Gaba, for soft eyes and dancing to *Butterflies*. Gabriel, for truly seeing people; and for sharing my love of Alpro yoghurt. City Boy, for being a new and necessary friend I didn't know I needed; you got Busy B*tch through her book. Phuong, for being a robot, but always making time to talk about love. Ujeza, for accepting me as I am, always. Niklas, for unwavering moral support, Brammibals Donuts and *kuscheln mit mir*. My roomies, friends and loves, you witnessed the day-to-day pain of this book. I could not have done it without your red bean bungeoppang, debriefs and love.

For all my Minerva friends, who taught me that home is not a place, but a community. For Berlin, for Seoul, for Jeju Island, for the hectic homes I found between putting words to page. For Amy, because you believed I could write a book from the first second I mentioned it. For Mike, who was my first real author friend and was always a supportive email away. For the friends I met on my travels who helped teach me who I am; Shammy, Ananya, Phoebe, Fraser Island Family.

Sixteenth, you guys are family. Danny, you're my big brother; thank you for taking a chance on a bushy-haired teen back in Timberyard, you changed my life. Mama Rach, if a hug was a human, it would be you, I adore you. Nish, you are my hype woman and you got me through this book.

My success on YouTube was not a solo endeavour. The wonderful StudyTube community is called a community for a reason. For Eve Bennett and Ruby Granger, who pioneered this online space with me back in sixth form and made me embrace my love of studying — look where we are now! Jack, you were one of the first people I told about this book and your unwavering support got me through; thank you for sending me random poems when I was at my lowest. Eve, you have a talent of always making me feel like I can do anything. Vee, I could not have chosen a better friend to write a book alongside, thank you for our 2am-writing-and-hype chats. For all the other icons who shared their advice in this book, and who I am fortunate enough to call not only my role models, but my friends: Ali, Holly, Renee, Paige, Viola, Mani, Ehis; you inspire me every day.

And when they say it takes a village to write a book, they're right — whoever 'they' are. A huge thank you goes to my editor and cheerleader Madiya. I called this woman every two weeks for nine months straight. She saw my tears, my rock-bottom burnout and talked me out of giving up more often than I care to admit. For the whole team at Bonnier Books UK for making my dream a reality: Ali, Eleanor, Sophie.

And of course, this book would not have been written without mugfuls of herbal tea, yoga sessions with Yoga with Adriene and Patrick, my beloved Lo-fi beats playlist and coffee. Lots of coffee. When I first started writing this book, I didn't like coffee. Now I love it so much that it gets its own line in the acknowledgements.

But the biggest thank you of all goes to my YouTube audience and online community without whom StudyTube and this book would never have happened. You utterly changed my life and I will forever be grateful. I hope you feel like every one of your dreams are within reach. If I can do it, you can too.

ABOUT THE AUTHOR

Jade Bowler is one of the very first StudyTubers, pioneering an online movement to inspire students around the world to improve in their studies while looking after their mental wellbeing.